John Adams

A collection of State-Papers

Relative to the first acknowledgement of the sovereignity of the United

States of America: and the reception of their minister plenipotentiary, by

their high mightinesses of the States-General of the United Netherlands

John Adams

A collection of State-Papers
*Relative to the first acknowledgement of the sovereignity of the United States of
America: and the reception of their minister plenipotentiary, by their high
mightinesses of the States-General of the United Netherlands*

ISBN/EAN: 9783337218447

Printed in Europe, USA, Canada, Australia, Japan

Cover: Foto ©Suzi / pixelio.de

More available books at **www.hansebooks.com**

A COLLECTION

O F

STATE-PAPERS,

Relative to the firſt Acknowledgment of the Sovereignity of the United States of Aмеrica,
and the reception of their Miniſter Plenipotentiary, by their High-Mightinesfes the States - General of the United Netherlands.

___

AT THE HAGUE,

MDCCLXXXII.

MEMORIAL

To their High-Mightinesses, the States-General of the United Provinces of the Low-Countries.

High and Mighty Lords,

The Subfcriber has the honour, to propofe to your High-Mightinefsfes, that the United States of America, in Congrefs affembled, have lately thought fit to fend him a Commiffion (with full Powers and Inftructions) to confer with your H. M. concerning a Treaty of Amity and Commerce , an authentic Copy of which he has the honour to annex to this Memorial.

At the times when the Treaties between this Republick and the Crown of Great-Britain were made, the People, who now compofe the United States of America , were a Part of the Englifh Nation; as fuch, Allies of the Republick, and Parties to thofe Treaties; entitled to all their Benefits, and fubmitting chearfully to all their Obligations.

It is true, that when the British Adminiftration, renouncing the ancient Character of Englishmen for Generofity, Juftice and Humanity , conceived the defign of fubverting the political Syftems of the Colonies; depriving them of the Rights and Liberties of Englishmen, and reducing them to the worft of all Forms of Government, ftarving the People by blockading the Ports, and cutting off their Fifheries and Commerce ; fending Fleets and Armies to deftroy every principle and fentiment of Liberty, and to confume their Habitations and their Lives; making Contracts for foreign Troops, and Alliances with favage Nations to affift them in their Enter-

prife,

prife; cafting formally, by Act of Parliament, three Millions of People at once out of the protection of the Crown: then, and not till then, did the United States of America, in Congrefs affembled, pafs that memorable Act, by which they affumed an equal Station among the Nations.

Thi immortal Declaration, of the 4 of July 1776, when America was invaded by an hundred Vefsels of War, and, according to Eftimates laid before Parliament, by 55,000 of veteran Troops, was not the effect of any fudden Paffion, or Enthufiasm; but a meafure which had been long in deliberation among the People, maturely discusfed in fome hundreds of popular Affemblies, and by public Writings in all the States: it was a meafure which Congrefs did not adopt until they had received the pofitive Inftructions of their Conftituents in all the States: it was then unanimously adopted by Congrefs, fubfcribed by all its Members, transmitted to the Affemblies of the feveral States, and by them refpectively accepted, ratified and recorded among their Archives; fo that no Decree, Edict, Statute, Placart or fundamental Law of any Nation was ever made with more Solemnity, or with more Unanimity or Cordiality adopted, as the Act and Confent of the whole People, than this: and it has been held facred to this day by every State, with fuch unshaken firmnefs, that not even the fmalleft has ever been induced to depart from it: although the English have wafted many Millions, and vaft Fleets and Armies, in the vain Attempt to invalidate it. On the contrary, each of the thirteen States has inftituted a form of government for itfelf under the Authority of the People; has erected its Legislature in the feveral Branches; its Executive Authority with all its Offices; its Judiciary departments and Judges;

ges; its Army, Militia, Revenue, and fome of
them their Navy: and all thofe departments of
Government have been regularly and conftitutionally
organized under the affociated Superintendency of
Congrefs, now thefe five years, and have acquired
a Confiftency, Solidity, and Activity equal to the
oldeft and moft eftablished Governments. It is
true, that in fome Speeches and Writings of the
English it is ftill contended, that the People of
America are ftill in principle and affection with
them: but thefe affertions are made againft fuch evident Truth and Demonftration, that it is furpri-
fing they fhould find at this day one believer in the
World. One may appeal to the Writings and recorded Speeches of the English for the laft feven-
teen years, to fhew, that fimilar misreprefentations
have been inceffantly repeated through that whole
Period, and that the Conclufion of every year has
in fact confuted the confident Affertions and Pre-
dictions of the beginning of it. The Subfcriber begs
leave to fay from his own Knowledge of the People of America, (and he has a better Right to obtain credit, becaufe he has better opportunities to
know, than any Briton whatfoever) that they are
unalterably determined to maintain their Independence. He confeffes, that notwithftanding his Confidence through his whole Life in the virtuous Senti-
ments and Uniformity of Character among his Coun-
trymen, their Unanimity has furprifed him: that all
the Power, Arts, Intrigues and Bribes, which have been employed in the feveral States, fhould have feduced from the Standard of Virtue, fo contemptible a few, is more fortunate than could have
been expected. This Independence ftands upon
fo broad & firm a bottom of the peoples interefts,
honour, confciences & affections, that it will not
be affected by any Succeffes the English may ob-

tain

tain either in America, or againſt the European Powers at War, nor by any Alliances they can poſſi-
bly form; if indeed in ſo unjuſt & deſperate a Cauſe
they can obtain any. Nevertheleſs, altho compelled by Neceſſity, & warranted by the fundamental
Laws of the Colonies, and of the British Conſtitution,
by principles avowed in the English Laws, and con-
firmed by many Examples in the English Hiſtory,
by principles interwoven into the Hiſtory and public
Right of Europe, in the great Examples of the Hel-
vetic and Belgic Confederacies, and many others;
and frequently acknowledged and ratified by the
Diplomatic Body, principles founded in eternal Juſtice, and the Laws of God and Nature, to cut
aſunder for ever, all the Ties which had connected
them with Great Britain: yet the People of America did not conſider themſelves as ſeparating from
their Allies, eſpecially the Republic of the United
Provinces, or departing from their connexions
with any of the People under their Government;
but, on the contrary, they preſerved the ſame
Affection, Eſteem and Reſpect for the Dutch Nation, in every part of the World, which they and
their Anceſtors had ever entertained.

When ſound policy dictated to Congreſs the pre-
caution of ſending Perſons to negotiate natural Alliances in Europe, it was not from a failure in
Reſpect that they did not ſend a Miniſter to your
High-Mightineſſes, with te firſt whom they ſent
abroad: but, inſtructed in the Nature of the Connections between Great-Britain and the Republic,
and in the ſyſtem of peace and Neutrality, which
ſhe had ſo long purſued, they thought proper to
reſpect both ſo far, as not to ſeek to embroil her
with her Allies, to excite diviſions in the Nation,
or lay Embarraſsments before it. But, ſince the
British Adminiſtration, uniform and perſevering in

In-

Injuſtice, defpiſing their Allies, as much as their
Coloniſts and Fellow - ſubjects ; disregarding the
Faith of Treaties, as much as that of Royal Char-
ters; violating the Law of Nations, as they had before done the fundamental Laws of the Colonies
and the inherent Rights of British ſubjects, have
arbitrarily ſet aſide all the Treaties between the
Crown and the Republic, declared War and commenced Hoſtilities, the ſettled Intentions of which
they had manifeſted long before ; all thoſe Motives, which before reſtrained the Congreſs, ceaſe:
and an Opportunity preſents of propoſing ſuch Connections, as the United States of America have a
Right to forme, conſiſtent with the Treaties already formed with France & Spain, which they are
under every Obligation of Duty, Intereſt and Inclination to obſerve ſacred and inviolate; and conſiſtent with ſuch other Treaties, as it is their Intention to propoſe to other Sovereigns.

If there was ever among Nations a natural Alliance, one may be formed between the two Re-
publics. The firſt planters of the four northern
States found in this Country an Aſylum from Per-
ſecution, and reſided here from the Year one thou-
ſand ſix hundred and eight to the Year one thou-
ſand ſix hundred and twenty, twelve Years prece-
ding their Migration. They ever entertained and
have transmitted to Poſterity, a grateful Remembrance of that Protection and Hoſpitality, and es-
pecially of that religious Liberty they found here,
having ſought it in vain in England.

The firſt Inhabitants of two other States, New-
York and New-Jerſey, were immediate Emigrants
from this Nation, and have transmitted their Religion, Language, Cuſtoms, Manners and Character: and America in general, until her Connections

with the Houfe of Bourbon, has ever confidered this Nation as her firft Friend in Europe, whofe Hiftory, and the great Characters it exhibits, in the various Arts of Peace, as well as Atchievements of War by Sea and Land, have been particularly ftudied, admired and imitated in every State.

A Similitude of Religion, although it is not dee-med fo effential in this as in former Ages to the Alliance of Nations, is ftill, as it ever will be thought, a defirable Circumftance. Now it may be faid with Truth, that there are no two Nations, whofe Worfhip, Doctrine and Difcipline, are more alike than thofe of the two Republicks. In this particular therefore, as far as it is of weight, an Alliance would be perfectly natural.

A Similarity in the Forms of Government, is ufually confidered as another Circumftance, which renders Alliances natural: and although the Confti-tutions of the two Republicks are not perfectly ali-ke, there is yet Analogy enough between them, to make a Connection eafy in this refpect.

In general Ufages, and in the Liberality of Sen-timents in thofe momentous Points, the Freedom of Enquiry, the Right of private Judgment and the Liberty of Confcience, of fo much Importan-ce to be fupported in the World, and imparted to all Mankind, and which at this Hour are in more danger from Great Britain and that intolerant fpirit which is fecretly fomenting there, than from any other cuarter, the two Nations refemble each other more than any others.

The Originals of the two Republicks are fo much alike, that the Hiftory of one feems but a Tran-fcript from that of the other: fo that every Dutch-man inftructed in the fubject, muft pronounce the American Revolution juft and neceffary, or pafs

a

a Cenfure upon the greateſt Actions of his immortal Anceſtors: Actions which have been approved
and applauded by Mankind, and juſtified by the
Deciſion of Heaven.

But the Circumſtance', which perhaps in this
Age has ſtronger influence than any other in the
formation of Friendſhips between Nations, is the
great and growing Intereſt of Commerce ; of the
whole ſyſtem of which through the Globe, your
High-Mightineſſes are too perfect Maſters, for me
to ſay any thing that is not familiary known. It
may not however be amiſs to hint, that the cen-
tral ſituation of this Country, her extenſive Navigation, her Poſſeſſions in the Eaſt- and Weſt-Indies, the Intelligence of her Merchants, the Number of her Capitaliſts, and the Riches of her Funds,
render a Connection with her very deſirable to
America: and on the other Hand, the Abundance
and Variety of the Productions of America, the
Materials of Manufactures, Navigation and Commerce ; the vaſt Demand and Conſumption in
America of the Manufactures of Europe, of Mer-
chandiſes from the Baltic, and from the Eaſt-In-
dies, and the ſituation of the Dutch Poſſeſſions in
the Weſt-Indies, cannot admit of a doubt, that
a Connection with the United States would be uſeful to this Republic. The Engliſh are ſo ſenſible
of this, that notwithſtanding all their Profeſſions
of Friendſhip, they have ever conſidered this Nation as their Rival in the American Trade ; a Sentiment which dictated and maintained their ſevere
Act of Navigation, as injurious to the Commerce
and Naval Power of this Country, as it was both
to the Trade and the Rights of the Coloniſts.
There is now an Opportunity offered to both, to
ſhake off this ſhackle for ever. If any Conſideration

tion whatever could have induced them to have avoided a War with your High-Mightinesses, it would have been the Apprehension of an Alliance between the two Republicks: and it is easy to forefee, that nothing will contribute more to oblige them to a Peace, than such a Connection once completely formed. It is needless to point out particularly, what Advantages might be derived to the possessions of the Republick in the West Indies from a Trade opened, protected and encouraged between them and the Continent of America; or what Profits might be made by the Dutch East-India Company, by carrying their Effects directly to the American Market; or how much even the Trade of the Baltic might be secured and extended by a free Intercourse with America, which has ever had so large a demand, and will have more for Hemp, Cordage, Sail-Cloth and other Articles of that Commerce: how much the national navigation would be benefited by building & purchasing ships there: how much the number of seamen might be increased, or how much advantages to both Countries, to have their Ports mutually opened to their men of war & privateers & their Prises.

If therefore an Analogy of Religion, Government, Original, Manners, and the most extensive and lasting commercial Interests, can form a Ground and an Invitation to political Connections, the Subscriber flatters himself, that in all these Particulars the Union is so obviously natural, that there has seldom been a more distinct Designation of Providence to any two distant Nations to unite themselves together.

It is further submitted to the Wisdom and Humanity of your High-Mightinesses, whether it is not visibly for the good of Mankind, that the Powers
of

of Europe, who are convinced of the Juſtice of
the American Cauſe, (and where is one to be
found that is not?) ſhould make haſte to acknowledge the Independence of the United States, and
form equitable Treaties with them, as the ſureſt
means of convincing Great-Britain of the Impracti-
cability of her purſuits? whether the late Marine
Treaty concerning the Rights of neutral Veſſels,
noble and uſeful as it is, can be eſtablished againſt
Great-Britain, who will never adopt it, nor ſubmit
to it, but from Neceſſity, without the Independence of America? whether the Return of America,
with her Nurſeries of Seamen and Magazines of
Materials for Navigation and Commerce, to the
Domination and Monopoly of Great-Britain, if
that were practicable, would not put the Poſſeſſions
of other Nations beyond ſeas wholly in the Power
of that enormous Empire, which has been long governed wholly by the feeling of its own Power, at
leaſt without a proportional attention to Juſtice,
Humanity, or Decency. When it is obvious and
certain, that the Americans are not inclined to ſubmit again to the British Government, on the one
hand, and that the Powers of Europe ought not
and could not with ſafety conſent to it, if they were, on the other; why ſhould a Source of Con-
tention be left open, for future contingencies to
involve the Nations of Europe in ſtill more blood-
ſhed, when, by one deciſive ſtep of the Maritime
Powers, in making Treaties with a Nation long in
Poſſeſſion of Sovereignity by Right and in Fact, it
might be cloſed?

The Example of your High-Mightineſſes would,
it is hoped, be followed by all the Maritime Powers, eſpecially thoſe which are Parties to the late
Marine Treaty: nor can Apprehenſion, that the In-

de-

dependence of America would be injurious to the
Trade of the Baltick, be any Objection. This Jea-
loufy is fo groundlefs, that the reverfe would hap-
pen. The Freight and Infurance in Voyages acrofs
the Atlantic are fo high, and the Price of Labour
in America fo dear, that Tar, Pitch, Turpentine
and Ship Timber never can be transported to Europe at fo cheap a Rate, as it has been and will
be afforded by Countries round the Baltick. This
Commerce was fupported by the English before the
Revolution with difficulty, and not without large
Parlimentary Bounties. Of Hemp, Cordage and
Sail-Cloth there will not probably be a Sufficiency
raifed in America for her own Confumption in many Centuries, for the plaineft of all Reafons, becaufe thefe Articles may be imported from Amfterdam, or even from Petersbourg and Archangel,
cheaper than they can be raifed at home. America
will therefore be for Ages a Market for thefe Articles of the Baltic Trade.

Nor is there more folidity in another Suppofi-
tion, propagated by the English to prevent other
Nations from purfuing their true Interefts, that the
Colonies of other Nations will follow the Example
of the United States. Thofe Powers, who have as
large Pofsesfions as any beyond feas, have already
declared againft England, apprehending no fuch
Confequences. Indeed there is no probability of
any other Power of Europe following the Example
of England, in attempting to change the whole Syftem of the Government of Colonies, and reducing
them by Oppreffion to the Neceffity of governing
themfelves: and without fuch manifeft Injuftice and
Cruelty on the Part of the Metropolis, there is no
danger of Colonies attempting Innovations. Eftablished Governments are founded deep in the
Hearts

Hearts, the Paffions, the Imaginations and Under-
ftandings of the People; and without fome violent
Change from without, to alter the Temper and Character of the whole People, it is not in human Nature to exchange Safety for Danger, and certain
Happinefs for very precarious Benefits.

It is fubmitted to the Confideration of your High-
Mightinefses, whether the Syftem of the United
States, which was minutely confidered and difcuf-
sed, and unanimously agreed on in Congrefs in the
Year 1776, in planing the Treaty they propofed
to France, to form equitable commercial Treaties
with all the Maritime Powers of Europe, without
being governed or monopolized by any : a Syftem
which was afterwards approved by the King, and
made the foundation of the Treaties with his Ma-
jefty : a Syftem to which the United States have
hitherto conftantly adhered, and from which they
never will depart, unlefs compelled by fome Powers declaring againft them, which is not expected,
is not the only means of preventing this growing
Country from being an Object of everlafting Jealou-
fies, Rivalties and Wars among the Nations. If this
Idea is juft, it follows, that it is the Intereft of every
State in Europe to acknowledge American Indepen-
dency immediately. If fuch benevolent Policy fhould
be adopted, the new World will be a proportional Blefling to every Part of the old.

The Subfcriber has the further Honour of infor-
ming your H. M., that the United States of America, in Congrefs afsembled, imprefsed with an
high Senfe of the Wisdom and Magnanimity of your
H. M., and of your inviolable Attachment to the
Rights and Liberties of Mankind, and being defi-
rous of cultivating the Friendship of a Nation,
eminent for its Wisdom, Juftice and Moderation,
have

have appointed the Subfcriber to be their Minifter Plenipotentiary to refide near you, that he may give you more particular afurances of the great Refpect they entertain for your H. M., befeeching your H. M. to give entire Credit to every thing, which their faid Minifter fhall deliver on their Part, efpecially when he fhall afure You of the Sincerity of their Friendfhip and Regard. The original Letter of Credence, under the Seal of Congrefs, the Subfcriber is ready to deliver to your H. M., or to fuch Perfons as you fhall direct to receive it. He has alfo a fimilar Letter of Credence to his moft Serene Highnefs the Prince Stadtholder.

All which is refpectfully fubmitted to the Confideration of your H. M., together with the Propriety of appointing fome Perfon, or Perfons, to treat on the Subject of his Miffion, by

LEYDEN
19. April 1781,

J. ADAMS.

GUEL.

GUELDERLAND.

In the Affembly of the States of Guelderland
held in October 1781, to confider of the Requifition of the King of France, of a negotiation
of five millions of Florins, under te Warranty of
the Republick, fome were for an Alliance with
France. The Baron Nagel, Senechal of Zutphen, avoided putting of the Queftion, and faid
among other Things: „ That he had rather ac-
„ knowledge the Independence of the Ameri-
„ cans, than contract an Alliance with France ".
The Baron van der Capellen de Marfch was for
an alliance with France and America too, He
obferved „ That nothing being more natural than
to act in Concert with the Ennemies of our Ennemy, it was an object of ferious Deliberation, to
fee, if the Intereft of the Republick did not re-
quire to accept, without further Tergiverfations,
the Invitations and Offers of the Americans: that
no Condefcention for England could hinder Us,
at prefent, from uniting ourfelves, againft a common Ennemy, wit a Nation fo brave, and fo virtuous: a Nation, which after our Example, owes
its Liberty to its valour, and even at this moment
is employed, in defending itfelf from the Tyran-
ny of the Ennemy of the two Nations: that confequently, nothing could reftrain us from acknow.
ledging

ledging the Independence of this new Republick:
That our conduct differed very much, from that held
by our Anceftors, who allied themfelves with
the Portuguefe, as foon, as they fhook off the Yoke
of the Spaniards: That there was no doubt, that
the faid alliances with the Ennemies of our Ennemy
would foon reftrain his Fury, and operate a general Peace advantageous for us ".

THE

THE QUARTER

OF

OOSTERGO.

The Quarter of Ooftergo in the Province of Friesland, in December 1781, was the firft public Body, which propofed a Connection with the United States of America in thefe words.

Every impartial Patriot, has a long time perceived, that in the Direction of affairs relative to this war with England, there has been manifested an inconceivable Lukewarmnefs and Sloth: buth they discover themfelves ftill more, at this moment, by the little Inclination which, in general, the Regencies of the Belgick Provinces teftify to commence a Treaty of Commerce and Friendship with the new Republick of the thirteen United States of North-America; and to contract Engagements, at least during the Continuance of this common war with the Crowns of France and Spain. Neverthelefs, the Neceffity of thefe Meafures appears clearly, fince, according to our judgments, nothing was more natural, nor more conformable to found Policy, founded upon the Laws of the Nature the moft precife, than that this Republick, immediately after the formal declaration of war, by the English (not being yet able to do any thing by military Exploits, not being in a ftate of Defence fufficiently refpectable, to dare, at Sea, to oppofe one fleet or fquadron,

B

to

to our perfidious Ennemy) fhould have commenced by acknowledging, by a publick declaration,
the Independence of North America. This would
have been from that time the greateft ftep to
the Humiliation of England, and our own Reeftablishment, and by this meafure, the Republick would have proved her firm Refolution to act
with vigour. Every one of our Inhabitants, all
Europe, who have their eyes fixed upon Us, the
whole world expected, with juft reafon, this meafure from the Republick. It is true, that before
the formal Declaration of war, by England, one
might perhaps have alledged fome plaufible Reafons, to juftify, in fome degree, the Backward-
nefs in this great and interefting affair. But, as
at prefent Great Britain is no longer our fecret, but declared Ennemy, which diffolves all
the Connections between the two Nations; and
as it is the duty, not only of all the Regencies, but
alfo of all the Citizens of this Republick, to reduce, by all imaginable annoyances, this Ennemy fo
unjuft to reafon, and to force him, if poffible, to
conclude an honourable Peace; why fhould we
hefitate any longer, to ftrike, by this meafure fo
reafonable, the moft fenfible blow to the common
Ennemy? will not this delay occafion a fufpicion,
that we prefer the Intereft of our Ennemy to that
of our Country? North-America, fo fenfibly offen-
ded by the Refufal of her Offer; France and Spain,
in the midft of a war fupported with activity, muft
they not regard Us as the fecret Friends, and
Favourers, of their and our common Ennemy? Have they not Reafon to conclude from it, that our
Inaction ought to be lefs attributed to our weaknefs, than to our affection for England? will not
this opinion deftroy all Confidence in our Nation
here-

heretofore fo renouned in this refpect? and our
Allies, at this time natural, muft they not imagine,
that it is better to have in us declared Ennemies
than pretended Friends? and fhall we not be involved in a ruinous war, which we might have
rendered advantageous, if it had been well directed?
while on the other hand it is evident, that by a new
Connection with the States of North-America, by
Engagements at leaft during this war with France
and Spain, we fhall obtain, not only the Confidence of thefe formidable Powers, inftead of their
diftruft, but by this means we fhall moreover
place our Colonies in Safety, againft any Infult; we
fhall have a well grounded hope, of recovering,
with the aid of the allied Powers, our loft Poffes-
fions, if the English fhould make themfelves
mafters of them, and our Commerce at prefent
neglected, and fo fhamefully pillaged, would
reaffume a new Vigour; confidering that in fuch
cafe, as it is manifeftly proved by folid reafons,
this Republick would derive from this Commerce
the moft fignal Advantages. But, fince our Intereft excites us forcibly, to act in Concert with
the Ennemies of our Ennemy; fince the United
States of America invite us to it long ago; fince
France appears inclined to concert her military
operations with ours, although this Power has
infinitely lefs Intereft to ally itfelf with us, whofe
weaknefs manifeft itfelf in fo palpable a manner, than
we are to form an Alliance, the moft refpectable in the
Univerfe: it is indubitably the duty of every Regency, to promote it with all their Forces, and
with all the Celerity imaginable. To this end,
we have thought it our Duty, to lay it before your
noble Mightineffes, in the firme Perfuafion, that
the Zeal of your noble Mightineffes will be as

car-

earneſt as ours, to concur to the Accompliſhment
of this Point, which is for us of the greateſt Importance; that, conſequently, your noble Mightineſſes will not delay, to cooperate with Us, that,
upon this important ſubject, there may be made to
their High-Mightineſſes, a Propoſition ſo vigorous,
that it may have the deſired Succeſs: and that this
affair, of an Importance beyond all Expreſſion
for our common Country, may be reſolved and decided by Unanimous Suffrages and in Preference to
every particular Intereſt.

ULTERIOUR

ULTERIOUR ADDRESS.

On the 9th January 1782, *Mr.* ADAMS, *waited on the President* VAN DEN SANDHEUVEL, *and addressed him as follows.*

ON the fourth of May, I had the honour of a Conference with the President of their High-Mightinesses, in which I informed him, that I had received from the United States of America a Commission with full Powers and Instructions, to propose and conclude a Treaty of Amity and Commerce between the said United States of America, and the United Provinces of the Netherlands.

At the same Conference, I had the honour to demand an Audience of their High-Mightinesses, in order to present to them my Letters of Credence and full Powers.

The President assured me, that he would make Report of all that I had said to him, to their High-Mightinesses, in order that it might be transmitted to the several Members of the Souvereignty of this Country, for their Deliberations and Decisions. — I have not yet been honoured with an Answer. I now do myself the honour to wait on you, Sir, to demand, as I do, a Categorical Answer, that I may be able to transmit it to my Souvereign. ——

GUELDER-

GUELDERLAND.

In an Extraordinary Affembly of the County of Zutphen, held at Nimeguen the 23 of February 1782, the following Meafures were taken.

After the Report of the Committee of this Province to the Generality, laid this day upon the Table, relative to what paffed in the precedent Affembly, and after the Examination of an Extract of the Regifter of the Refolutions of their High-Mightineffes the States General of the Low Countries of the ninth of laft Month, in relation to the alteriour Addrefs of Mr. Adams to the Prefident of their High-Mightineffes, concerning the Prefentation of his Letters of Credence to their High-Mightineffes, in behalf of the United States of America, demanding a Categorick Anfwer, whereof the Lords the Deputies of the refpective Provinces have taken Copies; the Baron Robert Jasper van der Capellen de Marsch, firft by word of Mouth, and afterwards in writing, propofed, and infifted at the Affembly of this Quarter, that at prefent, an without delay, we fhould make a Point of Deliberation, and that we fhould make upon the Table the neceffary overture, conceived more at length, in the Advice of this Nobleman inferted in thefe terms.

NOBLE AND MIGHTY LORDS!

The fubfcriber judges, upon good grounds, and without fear of being contradicted, that he is

able

able to affirm, that it is more than time that we should give a serious attention to the offer, and the Invitation, in every sense honourable and advantageous for this Republick, of Friendship, and reciprocal Connections with the thirteen American Provinces, now become free at the point of the sword, in such sort, that the Categorical Answer demanded by their Minister Mr. Adams, may become a subject of the deliberations of your Grand-Mightinesses, and that you may decide as soon as possible, concerning their respective Interests. He judges, that he ought not to have any further scruple in this regard; and that the uncertain consequences of the Mediation offered by Russia cannot, when certain Advantages for this Republick are in question, hinder that, out of regard for an Ennemy, with whom we (however salutary the views of her Imperial Majesty are represented) cannot make any Peace, at the Expence of a Negligence so irreparable: That a longer delay, to unite ourselves to a Nation already so powerfull, will have for its Consequence, that our Inhabitants will loose the means of extending, in a manner the most advantageous, their Commerce and their Prosperity: That by the vigorous Prohibition to import English Manufactures into America, our Manufactures, by means of Precautions taken in time, will rise out of their state of Languor: And that, by delaying longer to satisfy the wishes of the Nation, her Leaders will draw upon them the Reproach, of having neglected and rejected the favourable offers of Providence: that on the contrary, by adopting these Measures, the essential Interests of this unfortunate People will be taken to heart.

The subscriber declaring, moreover, that he

will

will abandon this unpardonable Negligence of an
opportunity favourable for the Republick, to the
account of thofe whom it may concern; protefting
againft all the fatal Confequences, that a longer
Refufal of thefe neceffary Meafures, will certainly
occafion: whereupon he demanded, that for his
Difcharge, this Note fhould be inferted in the
Regifters of the Quarter.

Signed

R. J. VAN DER CAPELLEN.

This advice having been read, Mr. Jacob Adolf.
de Heekeren d'Enghuifen, Councellor and firft Maf-
ter of Accounts in Guelderland, Prefident at this
time of the Affembly of the Quarter, reprefented
to the faid Robert Jasper van der Capellen de
Marfch, that „ Although he muft agree to the
Juftice of all that he had laid down, befides feveral other reafons equally ftrong which occurred to
his Mind, the Deliberation upon the Point in
queftion appeared to him premature, confidering that
the Lords the States of Holland and Weft-Friefland
and of Zealand, as the principal Commercial Provinces, who are directly interefted, had not neverthelefs as yet explained themfelves in this regard;
confequently that it would not be fo convenient for
the States of this Dutchy and County, who are
not interefted in it, but in a confequential and
indirect manner, to form the firft their Refolutions in this refpect: For this Reafon he propofed to Confideration, whether it would not be
more proper to poftpone the deliberations upon
this matter, to a future opportunity.

Never-

Nevertheleſs, the beforementioned Robert Jaſ-
per van der Capellen de Marſch inſiſting, that the
voices ſhould be collected upon the Propoſition
and Advice in queſtion, and thereupon having deliberated, their noble Mightineſſes have thought
fit to reſolve, that although the Motives alledged
by this Nobleman in his advice, appear to merit
a ſerious Conſideration, nevertheleſs, for the reaſons before alledged, they judge, that they ought
to ſuſpend the Deciſion of it, untill the Commercial Provinces have formed their Reſolutions
concerning it: And that, upon the Requiſition of
Robert Jasper van der Capellen de Marſch, there
be delivered to him an Extract of the preſent,
upon one as well as the other.

Signed

HERM. SCHOMAKER.

PETITION of LEYDEN.

To the noble, great, and venerable Lords of the Grand Council of the City of Leyden.

The Underfigned, all Manufacturers, Merchants, and other Traders of this City, moft refpectfully give to underftand, that it is a truth, as melancholly, as it is univerfally known, that the declenfion of Manufactures, which all the well-difpofed Citizens have remarked with the moft lively grief, from the beginning of this Century, has increafed more and more for feveral years; and that this principal Branch of the fubfiftance of the good Citizens, has fallen into fuch a ftate of Languor, that our City, once fo flourifhing, fo populous, fo celebrated, on account of its Commerce and of its Trades, appears to be threatned with total Ruin; that the diminution of its Merchants Houfes, on one hand, and on the other, the total Lofs, or the fenfible decreafe of feveral Branches of Commerce, furnifh an evident Proof of it; which the Petitioners could demonftrate by feveral Examples, if there were need of them to convince. Your noble and grand Lordfhips, to whom the Increafe of the Multitude of the Poor, the deplorable fituation of feveral Families, heretofore in eafy Circumftances, the depopulation of the City, which one cannot obferve without Emotion in the ruins of feveral ftreets, once neat and well inhabited, are fully known, will recollect no doubt upon this occafion, with Grief, that this ftate of Languor muft appear fo much the more defperate, if your noble and grand Lordfhips

fhips will take into confideration, that in this decay of Trades and Manufactures, we find a new
reafon of their further fall, confidering, that from
the time that there is not continual Employment, and an uninterrupted Sale, the Workmen
defert in fuch manner, that when confiderable
commiffions arrive, we cannot find capable hands,
and we fee ourfelves entirely out of a condition
to execute thefe orders.

That the Petitioners, with all the true Friends
of their country, extreamely affected with this al-
larming Situation of fo rich a Source of the publick Profperity, have indeed fought the means of
a Remedy, in amending fome defects, from which
it feemed to arife at leaft in Part; but that the meafures taken in this view, as is well known to your
noble and grand Lordships, have not had the defired Effect; at leaft, that they have not produced
a Reeftablishment fo effectual, that we have been
able to cbferve a fenfible Influence in the increafe of the fales of the manufactures of Leyden, as
appears moft evidently, by a comparifon of the
Pieces fabricated here, which have been heretofore carried to the diverfe markets of this City,
with thofe which are carried there at this day; a
comparifon which a true Citizen cannot confider
without regret.

That Experience has alfo taught the Petitioners,
that the principal Caufe of the decay of the manufactures of Holland, particularly thofe of Leyden, is not to be found in any internal vice either
in the capacity, or the Oeconomy of the Inhabitants, but in circumftances, which have happened abroad, and to which it is, confequently,
beyond the Power of the Petitioners, or of any
Citizen whatfoever to provide a remedy. That we
might

might cite, for example, the commerce of our
manufactures with Dantzick, and, through that
commercial City, with all Poland; a commerce,
which was carried on with fuccefs and advantage heretofore in our city, but is abfolutely in-
terrupted at this day, and vanished, by the revolution which has happened in that kingdom, and
by the burthenfome duties, to which the navigation of the Viftula has been fubjected. But that,
without entering into a detail of fimilar particular
fhackles, of which we might rekon a great number, the principal Caufe of the languishing ftate
of our manufactures confifts in the jealous Emulation of the neighbouring Nations, or rather of
all the People of Europe, confidering, that in this
age, the feveral Princes and Governments, enlightened in the real Sources of the publick Prosperity, and the true Interefts of their Subjects,
attach themfelves with Emulation, to revive in
their Kingdoms and States the national Induftry,
Commerce, and Navigation; to encourage them,
and promote them even by exclufive Priviledges,
or by heavy Impofitions upon foreign Merchandizes; Priviledges and Impofitions, which tend
equally to the Prejudice of the commerce and the
manufactures of our Country, as your noble & grand
Lordships will eafily recollect the Examples in
the Auftrian States and elfewhere. That in the
midft of thefe Powers and Nations, emulous or
jealous, it is impoffible for the citizens of our
Republick, however fuperiour their manufactures
may be in quality and finenefs, to refift a rivalry
fo univerfal, efpecially confidering the dearnefs
of Labour, caufed by that of the means of fubfi-
ftence; which in its turn is a neceffary confequence of the Taxes and Impofts, which the Inhabitants

of

of this State pay in a greater number, and a
higher rate, than in any other country, by reafon of
her natural fituation, and of its means to fupport
itfelf; fo that by the continual operation of this
principal, but irreparable caufe of decline, it is to
be feared, that the impoverishment, and the diminution of the good Citizens increafing with the
want of Employment, the Dutch Nation, heretofore the Purveyor of all Europe, will be obliged
to content itfelf with the Sale of its own Productions in the interiour of the country (and
how much does not even this Refource fuffer, by
the importation of foreign manufactures?) and that
Leyden, lately fo rich and flourishing, will exhi-
bit defolated quarters in its declining ftreets, and
its multitude, disgraced with want and mifery, an
affecting Proof of the fudden fall of Countries
formerly overflowing with profperity.

That, if we duely confider thefe motives, no
Citizen whofe heart is upright (as the Petitioners
affure themfelves) much lefs your noble and grand
Lordships, whofe good difpofitions they acknowledge with Gratitude, will take it amifs, that
we have fixed our eyes on the prefent Conjunc-
ture of affairs, to enquire, whether thefe times
might not furnish them fome means of reviving
the languishing Manufactures of Leyden; and that
after a Confideration well matured, they flatter
themfelves with the hope (a hope which unpreju-
diced Men will not certainly regard as a vain Chi-
mera) that in fact, by the prefent Circumftances,
there opens in their favour an Iffue, for arriving
at the Reeftablishment defired.

That from the time, when the Rupture between Great-Britain and the Colonies upon the
Continent of North-America appeared to be irre-
para-

parable, every attentive Spectator of this Event
perceived, or at least was convinced, that this
Rupture, by which there was born a Republick
as powerfull as industrious in the new World,
would have the most important Confequences for
Commerce and navigation, and that the other
commercial Nations of Europe would foon fhare
in a very confiderable Commerce, whereof the
Kingdom of Great Britain had referved to itfelf,
untill that time, the exclufive Poffeffion by its Act
of Navigation, and by the other Acts of Parliament prescribed to the Colonies; that in the time of it, this Reflection did not escape your Petitioners, and they foresaw, from that time, the
advantage which might arife in the fequel, from a
Revolution fo important for the United Provinces
in general, and for their native City in particular. But that they fhould have been afraid, to have placed this favorable Occafion before the
eyes of your noble and grand Lordships, at an
Epocha when the relations, which connected our
Republick with Great Britain her Neighbour,
feemed to forbid all Meafures of this nature, or
at leaft ought to make them be confidered as out
of feafon.

That, in the mean time, this reafon of Silence
has entiroly ceafed by the Hoftilities, which the
faid Kingdom has commenced againft our Republick, under Pretences, and in a manner, the Injuftice of which has been demonftrated by the fupream Government of the State, with an irrefra-
gable Evidence, in the eyes of impartial Europe;
whilft the Petitioners themfelves, by the illegal
Captore of fo large a number of Dutch Ships,
and afterwards by the abfolute Stagnation of navigation, and of Voyages to foreign Countries,
have

have experienced, in the moſt grievous manner, the conſequences of this hoſtile and unforeseen Attack, and feel them ſtill every day, as is abundantly known to your noble and grand Lordships. That ſince that Epocha, a ſtill more conſiderable number of Workmen muſt have remained without Employment, and ſeveral Fathers of Families have quitted the City, abandoning, to the further Expence of the Treaſury of the Poor, their Wives and their Children plunged in Miſery.

That during this Rupture, which has ſubſiſted now for fifteen months, there has occurred another Circumſtance, which has encouraged the Petitioners ſtill more, and which to them appears to be of ſuch a nature, that they would be guilty of an exceſſive Indifference, and an unpardonable Negligence towards the City, towards the lower Claſs of Inhabitants, towards their own Families, and towards themſelves, if they ſhould delay any longer, to lay open their Intereſts to your noble and grand Lordships, in a manner the moſt reſpectfull, but the moſt energick; to wit, that the United States of America have very rigorously forbid, by a reſolution of Congreſs agreed to in all the thirteen States, the Importation of all Engliſh manufactures, and in general, all the merchandizes fabricated in the Dominions which yet remain to Great-Britain. That the Effect of this Prohibition muſt neceſſarily be a Spirit of Emulation between all the commercial nations, to take place of the British Merchants and Manufacturers in this important Branch of Exportation, which is entirely cut off from them at this day. That neverthelefs, among all the nations there is none, which can entertain a hope, better founded, and more ſure, in this reſpect, than the Citizens of this free
Repu-

Republick, whether on account of the Identity of Religion, the fashion of Living, the manners, whether becaufe of the Extent of its commerce, and the convenience of its navigation, but above all, by reafon of the Activity and good faith, which ftill diftinguishes (without boafting too much) the Dutch Nation above all other People; qualities in confideration of which, the Citizens of United America are inclined even at prefent, to prefer, in equal Circumftances, the Citizens of our free States, to every other nation.

. That, neverthelefs, all Relations and Connec-tions of Commerce between the two Peoples, can-not but be uncertain and fluctuating, as long as their offers and reciprocal Engagements are not fixed and regulated by a Treaty of Commerce. That at this day, if ever, (according to the refpectfull opinion of the Petitioners) there exifts a neceffity the moft abfolute, for the Conclufion of a fimilar Treaty of Commerce, there, where we may fay with Truth, that there arifes for the Republick, for our Leyden efpecially, a moment, which once efcaped, perhaps never will return, fince the national Affembly of Great Britain, convin-ced by a terrible and fatal Experience, of the ab-folute Impoffibility of reattaching united Ame-rica to the British Crown, has laid before the Throne its defire to conclude a neceffary Peace with a People, free as this day at the Price of their Blood: So that if this Peace fhould be once concluded, the Dutch Nation would fee itfelf perhaps excluded from all Advantages of Commerce with this new Republick, or at leaft would be treated by her with an Indifference, which the fmall value, which we fhould have put

upon

upon its Friendship in former times, would feem
to merit.

That, fuppofing for a moment, that a Peace,
between England and United America, were
not fo near, as we have reafon to prefume not
without probability, there would be found in that
cafe nations enough, who will be jealous of ac-
quiring, after the example of France, the earlieft
right to Commerce with a Country, which already
peopled by feveral Millions of Inhabitants, augments
every day in Population, in a manner incredible,
but, as a new People, unprovided as yet with
feveral neceffary Articles, will procure a rich,
even an immenfe Outlet, for the Fabricks and
Manufactures of Europe.

That, however manifeft the Intereft, which the
Petitioners and all the Citizens of Leyden would
have in the Conclufion of fuch a Treaty of Commerce, they would however have made a fcruple,
to lay before the paternal eyes of your noble
and grand Lordships, the utility or rather the neceffity of fuch a meafure, in refpect to them, if
they could believe, that their particular Advantage would be, in any wife, contrary to the more
univerfal Interefts of all the Republick. But, as
far as the Petitioners may judge, as Citizens, of
the Situation, and the political Exiftence of their
Country, they are ignorant of any reafons of this
kind: but, on the contrary, they dare appeal
to the unanimous voice of their fellow - Citizens,
well intentioned, in the other Cities and Provinces, even of the Regents the moft diftinguished;
fince it is univerfally known, that the Province of
Friefland has already preceeded the other Confederates by a Refolution, for opening negotiations with America; and that in other Provinces,

C   which

which have an Interest less direct in Commerce
and Manufactures, celebrated Regents appear
to wait merely for the example of the Commercial
Provinces, for taking a similar Resolution.

That the Petitioners will not detain the attention
of your noble and grand Mightinesses, by a more
ample detail of their Reasons and Motifs, since,
on one hand, they assure themselves, that these
reasons and motifs will not escape the enlightened and attentive Judgment of your grand and noble Lordships, and on the other, they know by
experience, that your grand and noble Lordships
are disposed, not to suffer any occasion to pass, for
promoting the welbeing of their City, for advan-
cing the Prosperity of the Citizens, to render their
names dear to their Contemporaries, and make
them blissed by Posterity.

In which firm expectation, the Petitioners address themselves to this grand Council with the
respectfull but serious Request, that it may please
your noble and great Lordships, to direct, by their
powerfull Influence, things in such sort, that in
the Assembly highly respected of their noble and
grand Mightinesses the Lords the States of Holland and Westfriesland, there be opened deliberations, or, already opened, carried as speedily as
possible to an effectual Conclusion, such as they
shal find the most proper, for obtaining the law-
full End, and fullfilling the Desires of the Petitioners, or as they shall judge conformable to the
general Interest.

So doing &c.

LEYDEN

L E Y D E N.

*An Address of Thanks, with a
further Petition.*

To the noble, great, and venerable Lords, the
great Council of the City of Leyden.

The underfigned Manufacturers, Merchants and
other Traders, interefted in the Manufactures and
Fabricks of this City, give refpectfully to underftand.

That a number of the Underfigned, having taken, the 18 of March, the liberty to prefent, to
your noble and great Lordships, a refpectfull Requeft, to obtain the Conclufion of Connections of
Commerce with United America ,, the Petitioners
judge that they ought to hold it for a duty, as agreable as indifpenfible, to teftify their fincere Gratitude, not only for the gracious manner, in which
your noble and great Lordships have been pleafed to accept that requeft, but alfo for the Patriotic Refolution that your noble and great Lordships have taken upon its object; a Refolution,
in virtue of which the City of Leyden (as the
Petitioners have the beft reafons to fuppofe) hath
been one of the first Cities of this Province, from
whofe Unanimous Cooperation has originated the
Refolution of their noble and grand Mightineffes of
the date of the 28 of March laft " to direct things
on the Part of their noble and grand Mightineffes,
in the Affembly of the States General, and to
make there the ftrongeft Inftances, to the end,
C 2   that

that Mr. Adams may be admitted and acknowledged as Minister of the United States of America".

That the Petitioners regard, with all honesthearted Citizens, the present Epocha, as one of the moſt glorious in the Annals of our dear Country, feeing that there has been manifeſted, in a moſt fignal manner, on one hand, a Confidence the moſt cordial of the good Citizens towards their Regents, on the other a paternal Attention and Deference of the Regents to the refpectfull but well founded Prayers of their faithfull Citizens, and, in general, the moſt exemplary Unanimity, throughout the whole Nation, to the Confufion of thoſe, who, having endeavoured to fow the feeds of Discord, would have rejoiced if they could fay with truth, that a Diſſention fo fatal had rooted itfelf, to the Ruin of the Country and of the People.

That the Petitioners, feeling themfelves penetrated, with the moſt pleafing Emotions, by an Harmony fo Univerfal, cannot pafs over in Silence the Reflection, that your noble and great Lordfhips, taking a Refolution the moſt favourable, upon the faid Requeſt, have difcovered thereby, that they would not abandon the footſteps of their Anceſtors, who found in the united fentiments of Magiſtrates and Citizens, the Refources neceſſary to refiſt a powerfull oppreſſor, who even would not have undertaken that difficult, but glorious Task, if they had not been fupported by the voice of the moſt refpectable Part of the Nation.

That encouraged by this Reflection, the Petitioners affure themfelves, that your noble and great Lordships will honour, with the fame Approbation

tion, the ſtep, which they take to day, to recommend to your noble and great Lordſhips, in a manner the moſt reſpectfull, but at the ſame time the moſt preſſing, the promt and efficacious Execution of the aforeſaid Reſolution of their noble and grand Mightineſſes of the 28 of March laſt, with every thing which depends thereon; a Proceeding, which does not ſpring from a deſire, on the part of the Petitioners, to raiſe themſelves above the ſphare of their duties and vocations, or to interfere, indiſcreetly, the affairs of Government, but only from a Conviction, that it cannot but be agreable to well intentioned Regents (ſuch as your Noble and great Lordſhips, have ſhewn yourſel-ves by Deeds to your good Citizens) to ſee themſelves applauded in their ſalutary Efforts and patriotick Deſigns, and ſupported againſt the perverſe views, and ſecret machinations of the ill diſpoſed, who, however ſmall their Number, are always found in a nation.

That, although the Petitioners may be convinced, that their noble and grand Mightineſſes, having taken a Reſolution ſo agreable to all true Patriots, will not neglect to employ means to carry it to an efficacious Concluſion among the other Confederates, and to procure to the good Citizens, the real Enjoyment of the Commerce with United America, they cannot, nevertheleſs, diſſemble, that lately ſome new Reaſons have ariſen, which make them conceive ſome fears reſpecting the prompt Conſummation of this deſirable affair.

That the Probability of an offer of Peace, on the part of Great-Britain, to United America, whereof the Petitioners made mention in their former Requeſt, having at preſent become a full Certainty by the Revolution arrived ſince in the Britiſh

Miniſtry, they have not learned without Uneaſineſs
the attempt made at the ſame time by the new Mi-
niſters of the Court of London, to involve this
State, in a Negotiation for a ſeparate Peace, the
immediate Conſequence of which would be (as
the Petitioners fear) a Ceſſation of all Connections
with the American Republick, whilſt that in the
mean time our Republick, deprived on the one hand of
the Advantages, which it reaſonably promiſes itſelf from theſe Connections, might on the other
hand be detained by Negotiations, ſpun out to a
great Length, and not effect till late, perhaps
after the other belligerent Powers, a ſeparate Peace with England.

' That in effect the Difficulties, which oppoſe
themſelves to a like partial Pacification, are too
multipleid for one, to promiſe himſelf to ſee them
ſuddenly removed, ſuch as the Reſtitution of the
Poſſeſſions taken from the State, and retaken from
the Engliſh by France, a Reſtitution, which is
become thereby impracticable, the Indemnification
of the immenſe Loſſes, that, the unexpect.d and
perfidious Attack of England hath cauſed to the
Dutch Nation in general, to the Petitioners in
particular; the Aſſurance of a free Navigation, for
the future, upon the Principles of the armed Neutrality, and conformably to the Law of Nations;
the Diſſolution of the Bonds, which, without
being productive of any Utility to the two Nations, have been a ſource of Conteſtations, always
ſpringing up, and which, in every war between
Great Britain and any other Power, have threatned to involve our Republick in it, or have in
effect done it; the Annihilation, if poſſible, of the
act of Navigation, an act, which carries too evident

dent marks of the fupremacy affeéted by England
over all other maritime People, not to attraét Attention, at the approaching Negotiation of Peace;
finally, the Neceffity of breaking the yoke, that
Great Britain would impofe on our Flagg, to make
hers refpeéted in the northern Ocean, as the feat
of her maritime Empire; and other objeét- of this
Nature, which, as the petulant Proceedings of the
Court of London have given rife to them, will
certainly furnifh matter for Claims and Negotiations.

That, as by thefe Confiderations a fpeedy
Confummation of a feparate Peace with England
is out of all Probability, efpecially when one com-
pares with them the dubious and limited manner,
in which it is offered; on the other hand a general
Peace appears not to be fo for diftant, as that
to obtain a more prompt Reconciliation with England, the Republick hath occafion to abandon its
Interefts relative to North America, feeing that
the British Government hath refolved, upon the
Requeft of the national Affembly, even to discon-
tinue offenfive Hoftilities againft the new Republick; and that even under the prefent Adminiftration of the new Minifters, it appears ready
to acknowledge pofitively its Independence; an
acknowledgment, which, in removing the principal ftumbling Block of a Negotiation of a general
Peace, will pave the way to a prompt Explica-
tion of all the Difficulties between the Belligerent Powers.

That the Petitioners fhould exceed much the
Bounds of their Plan, if they entered into a more
ample detail of the Reafons which might be alledged upon this fubjeét, and which certainly will

not

not efcape the political Penetration of your noble
and great Lordships, among others, the Engagements recently entered into with the Court of
France, and which will not be violated by our
Republick, which acknowledges the fanctity of
its Engagements, and refpects them; but which
will ferve much rather to convince the Emprefs of
Ruffia of the Impoffibility of entering, in the prefent Juncture of Affairs, into fuch a Negociation,
as the Court of London propofes, when even it
will not be permitted to prefume, but that Sovereign will feel herfelf the Change of Circumftances, which have happened with regard to America fince the offer of her Mediation, by the Revolution in the Britifh Miniftry, and that fhe ought
even to regard a feparate Peace between our State
and England, as the moft proper mean to retard
the general Tranquility, that fhe hath endeavoured
to procure to all the Commercial Nations now in
war.

   That from thefe Motives the Petitioners refpectfully hope, that the aforefaid offer of England
will occafion no obftacle, which may prevent,
that the Refolution of their noble and grand Mightineffes, to acknowledge the Independence of
North America, and to conclude with that Power
a Treaty of Commerce, may not have a prompt
Execution, nor that even one only of the other
Confederates will fuffer itfelf to be diverted thereby from the defign of opening unanimoufly with
this Province, and the others which have declared
themfelves conformably with Holland, Negotiations with the United States, and of terminating
them as foon as poffible.

   That the favourable Refolutions, already taken
for this effect in Zeeland, Utrecht, Overysfel,
                        and

and at prefent (as the Petitioners learn) in the
Province of Groningen after the Examples of Holland and Friesland, confirm them in that hope,
and feem to render entirely fuperfluous, a Requeft,
that in every other Cafe the Petitioners would
have found themfelves obliged to make with the
commercial Citizens of the other Cities, to the
end, that by the Refiftance of one Province, not
immediately interefted in Commerce and Navigation, they might not be deprived of the Advantages and of the Protection, that the fovereign
Affembly of their proper Province had been dis-
pofed to procure them, without that, but that, to
the end to provide for it, their noble and grand
Mightineffes, and the States of the other Provinces in this refpect, Unanimous with them, fhould
make ufe of the Power, which belongs to each
free State of our federative Republick, at leaft in
regard to Treaties of Commerce, of which there
exifts an Example in 1649, not only in a Treaty
of Redemption of the Toll of the Sound, but
alfo, in a defenfive Treaty concluded with the
Crown of Denmark by the three Provinces of
Guelderland, Holland and Friesland.

But as every Apprehenfion of a fimilar Diffention,
among the members of the Confederation, appears
at prefent abfolutely unfeafonable, the Petitioners
will confine themfelves rather to another Requeft,
to wit, that after the formation of Connections
of Commerce with North America, the effectual
Enjoyment of it may be affured to the Commercial Citizens of this Country, by a fufficient Protection of their Navigation, without which the
Conclufion even of fuch a Treaty of Commerce
would be abfolutely illufory. That for a long time,
efpecially the laft year, the Petitioners have ta-

fted

fted the bitter Fruits of the defencelefs ftate, in
which the Dutch Flagg has been inceffantly found,
as they have already faid, conformably to the
truth, in their firft requeft, ,, that by the total
,, ftagnation of the Navigation, and of Expedi-
,, tions, they have felt in the moft painfull man-
,, ner, the effects of the hoftile and unexpected
,, Attack of Great Britain, and that they feel,
,, them ftill every day". That in the mean time
this ftagnation of Commerce, abfolutely abandoned
to the Rapacity of an Ennemy greedy of Pillage,
and deftitute of all Protection whatever, hath
appeared to the Petitioners, as well as to all the
other Commercial inhabitants, yes even to all true
Citizens, fo much the more hard and afflicting,
as they not only have conftantly contributed with
a good Heart, all the public Impofts, but that at
the time, even that the Commerce was abfolutely abandoned to itfelf, and deprived of all Safeguard, it fupported a double Charge to obtain that
Protection, which it hath never enjoyed, feeing
that the hope of fuch a Protection, (the Republick not being entirely without maritime Force)
hath appeared indeed more than once, but has always vanifhed in the moft unexpected manner, by
accidents and impediments, which, if they have
given rife, perhaps wrongfully, to difcontent and
to diftruft among the good Citizens, will not
neverthelefs be read and meditated by Pofterity
without furprize.

That, without Intention to legitimate, in any manner, the fufpicions arifing from this failure of Protection, the Petitioners believe themfelves, neverthelefs, with all proper refpect warranted, in addreffing
their Complaints on this head, to the Bofoms of your
noble and great Lordships, and (feeing that the
Com-

Commerce with North America cannot fubfift without Navigation, no more than Navigation without a Safeguard) in reckoning upon the active
Direction, the ufefull Employment, and prompt
Augmentation of our naval Forces, in Proportion
to the means, which fhall be the moft proper
effectually, to fecure to the Commerce of this
Republick the Fruits of its Connections with United North America.

For which Reafons, the Petitioners, returning
their folemn Thanks to your noble and great Lordfhips, for the favourable Refolution taken upon
their requeft the 18th. of March laft, addrefs themfelves anew to you, on this occafion, with the
refpectfull Prayer „ that it may gracioufly pleafe
„ your noble and great Lordships, to be willing
„ to effectuate by your powerfull Influence, whe-
„ ther in the illuftrious Affembly of their noble
„ and grand Mightineffes, whether among the other
„ Confederates, or elfewhere, there, and in fuch
„ manner as your noble and great Lordships
„ fhall judge moft proper, that the Refolution
„ of their noble and grand Mightineffes of the
„ date of the 28 of March laft, for the Ad-
„ miffion of Mr. Adams, in quality of Minifter
„ of the United States of America, be prompt-
„ ly executed, and that the Petitioners, with
„ the other Commercial Citizens, obtain the
„ effectual Enjoyment of a Treaty of Commerce
„ with the faid Republick, as well by the activity
„ of the Marine of the State, and the Protection
„ of Commerce and Navigation, as by all other
„ meafures, that your noble and great Lordships
„ with the other members of the Sovereign Go-
„ vernment of the Republick, fhall judge to
                                        „ tend.

„ tend to the public Good, and to ferve to the
„ Profperity of the dear Country, as well as
„ to the maintenance of its precious Liberties.

. *So doing &c.*

ROTTERDAM

ROTTERDAM.

PETITION *of the Merchants, Insurers,
and Freighters of Rotterdam to the
Regency of that City.*

GIVE to underſtand, in the moſt reſpectfull
manner, that it is ſufficiently notorious, that
the Inhabitants of this Republick have, as well
as any other Nation, an Intereſt, that they give
us an opportunity to open a free Communication
and Correſpondance with the Inhabitants of America, by making a Treaty of Commerce, as Mr.
Adams has repreſented in his Memorial; to which
they add, that the Advantages, which muſt re-
ſult from it, are abſolutely the only means of
reviving the fallen Commerce of this Country;
for reeſtablishing the Navigation, and for repai-
ring the great Damages, which the perfidious Proceedings of the English have, for ſo many years,
cauſed to the commercial Part of this Country.
That, with all due reſpect, they repreſent to
the venerable Regency the danger we run, in
prolonging further the deliberations, concerning
the Article of an alliance of Commerce with
North America; being moreover certain, that the
Interpoſition of this State cannot add any Thing
more to the ſolidity of its Independence, and
that the English Miniſtry has even made to the
Deputies of the American Congreſs Propoſitions,
to what Point they would eſtablish a Correſpondence there, to our Prejudice, and thereby depri-
ve

ve the Inhabitants of this Country of the certain
Advantages which might refult from this reciprocal Commerce; and that thus we ought not to
delay one day, nor even one hour, to try all the
efforts, that we may purſue the Negotiation offered by Mr. Adams, and that we may decide finally
upon it. Whereupon the Petitioners repreſent,
with all the reſpect poſſible, but at the ſame time
with the firmeſt Confidence, to the venerable Regency of this City, that they would authorize and
qualify the Lords their Deputies at the Affembly of their noble and grand Mightineſſes, to the
end, that they inſiſt in a manner the moſt
energic, at the Affembly of their noble and grand
Mightineſſes, that the Reſolution demanded may
be taken without the leaſt delay, to the end,
that, on the Part of this Province, it be effected
at the Affembly of the States General, that the
American Miniſter Mr. Adams be as ſoon as poſſible
admitted to the Audience which he has demanded, and that they take with him the determina-
tions neceſſary to render free and open to the
reciprocal Inhabitants, the Correſpondence demanded.

So doing &c.

THE PETITIONS *of the Merchants, and Manu-*
facturers of HAERLEM, LEIDEN *and* AM-
STERDAM, *which have been prefented on the
twentyeth of March to* THEIR HIGH-MIGH-
TINESSES, *were accompanied with an other
to the States of* HOLLAND *and* WEST-
FRIESLAND, *conceived in thefe Terms.*

THE Subfcribers, Inhabitants of this Country,
Merchants, Manufacturers, and others, living by Commerce, give with all refpect to underftand, that they have the honour to annex hereto
a Copy of a Petition prefented by them to their
High-Mightinesfes, the States General of the United Low-Countries. The Importance of the Thing
which it contains, the confiderable Commerce, which
thefe Countries might eftablish in North-America,
the Profits which we might draw from it, and the
Importance of Induftry and Manufactures, by the
relation which they have with Commerce in general, as well as the Navigation to that extenfive
Country; all thefe Objects have made them take
the liberty to reprefent, in the moft refpectfull
manner, this great affair for them and for the
Connections which the Petitioners may have, in
quality of Manufacturers, with the Merchants,
moft humbly praying your noble and grand Mightinesfes, for the acquifition of thefe important
Branches of Commerce, and for the advantage of
all the Manufactures, and other works of Labour
and of Trafick, to be fo good as to take this Petition, and the Reafons which it contains, into your
high

high Confideration, and to favour it with your powerfull Support and Protection, and by a favourable Refolution, which may be taken at the affembly of their High Mightineffes, to direct, on the Part of this Province, things in fuch a manner, that for obtaining this Commerce fo defired and fo neceffary for this Republick, that there be concerted fuch efficacious meafures, as the high wisdom and patriotic fentiments of your noble and grand Mightineffes may find convenient, for the welbeing of fo great a Numbre of Inhabitants, and for the Prejudice of their Ennemies.

So doing &c:

D O R.

DORDRECHT.

A T DORDRECHT there has not been presen-. ted any Petition. But on the twentyeth of March the Merchants, convinced by redoubled proofs of the Zeal, and of the Efforts of their Regency, for the true Interests of Commerce, judged it unneceſſary to preſent a Petition after the example of the Merchants of other Cities: they contended themſelves with teſtifying verbally their deſire, that there might be contracted connections of Commerce with the United States of America: that this ſtep had been crowned with ſuch happy ſucceſs, that the ſame day 20 March 1782, it was reſolved by the ancient Council, to authorize their Deputies at the Aſſembly of Holland, to concur in every manner poſſible, that, without delay, Mr. Adams be acknowledged in his Quality of Miniſter Plenipotentiary; that his Letters of Credence be accepted, and Conferences opened upon this object.

Z W O L L

IN OVERYSSEL.

THE Subfcribers, all Merchants, Manufacturers, and Factors of the City of Zwoll,
give refpectfully to underftand, that every one of
them, in his private concerns, finds by experience, as well as the Inhabitants of the Republick
in general, the grievous effects of the decay into
which Commerce, and the Manufactures of this
Country are fallen, little by little, and above all,
fince the hoftile attack of the Kingdom of England againft this State; that it being their duty
to their Country, as well as to themfelves, to
make ufe of all the circumftances which might
contribute to their reeftablishment, the Requifition made not long fince by Mr. Adams to the
Republick, to wit to conclude a Treaty of Commerce with the United States of North-America,
could not efcape their attention; an affair whofe
Utility, Advantage and Neceffity, for thefe Provinces, are fo evident, and fo often proved in
an inconteftible manner, that the Petitioners will
not fatigue your noble Lordships, by placing
them before you, nor the general Interefts of this
City, nor the particular Relations of the Petitioners, confidering that they are convinced, in the
firft place, that England making againft the Republick the moft ruinous war, and having bro-
ken every Treaty with her, all kind of Complai-
fance for that Kingdom is unfeafonable.

In

In the fecond Place, that America, which ought
to be regarded as become free at the point of the
fword, and as willing, by the Prohibition of all
the Productions and Manufactures of England, to
break abfolutely with that Kingdom; it is precifely
the time, and perhaps the only time, in which we
may have a favourable opportunity, to enter into
Connection with this new and powerfull Republick; a time which we cannot neglect without
running the greateft risque of being irrevocably
prevented by the other Powers, and even by
England. Thus we take the Liberty, refpectfully
to fupplicate your noble Lordships, that having
fhewn for a long time, that you fet a value upon
the formation of Alliances with powerfull States,
you may have the goodnefs, at the approaching
Affembly of the Nobility and of the Cities for-
ming the States of this Province, to redouble
your efforts, to the end, that in the name of this
Country it may be decided at the Generality,
that Mr. Adams be acknowledged, and the propofed Negotiations opened as foon as poffible,

So doing &c.

PETITION of AMSTERDAM.

To their High Mightinesses, the States General of the United Provinces, the undersigned, Merchants, Manufacturers and others, Inhabitants living by Commerce in this Country, give respectfully to understand:

That, although the Petitioners have always relyed, with entire confidence upon the Administration and the Resolutions of your High-Mightinesses, and it is against their Inclinations to interrupt your important deliberations, they think, however, that they ought, at this time, to take the Liberty, and believe as well intentioned Inhabitants, that it is their indispensable Duty in the present moment, which is most critical for the Republick, to lay humbly before your High-Mightinesses their Interests.

What good Citizen, in the Republick, having at heart the Interest of his dear Country, can dissemble, or represent to himself without dismay, the sad situation, to which we are reduced by the attack, equally sudden, unjust and perfidious of the English? who would have dared, two years ago, to foretell, and, notwithstanding the dark clouds, which even then began to form themselves, could even have imagined, that our Commerce, and our Navigation, with the immense affairs which depend upon them, the support and the prosperity of this Republick, could have fallen and remained in such a terrible decay? that in 1780, more than two thousands of Dutch vessells, having passed the Sound, not one was found upon
the

the Lift in 1781? That the Ocean, heretofore
covered with ourt veffells, fhould fee at prefent fcarcely any? and that we may be reduced to
fee our navigation, formerly fo much refpeéted
and preferred by all the nations, pafs entirely into
the hands of other Powers? It would be fuperfluous, to endeavour to explain at length, the
damages, the enormous loffes, which our Inhabitants have fuftained by the fudden Invafion, and
the Pillage of the Colonies, and of their fhips:
difafters, which not only fall directly upon the
Merchant, but which have alfo a general influence,
and make themfelves felt in the moft melancholly
manner, even by the loweft Artifans and Labou-
rers, by the languor which they occafion in Commerce. But, how great soever they may be, it
might perhaps be poffible, by the aid of the paternal cares of your High-Mightineffes, and by
oppofing a vigorous refiftance to the Ennemy,
already enervated, to repair in time all thefe
Loffes, (without mentioning Indemnifications) if
this ftagnation of Commerce was only momen-
tary, and if the induftrious Merchant did not fee
beforehand the fources of his future felicity dried
up. It is this gloomy forefight, which, in this
moment afflicts, in the higheft degree, the Petitioners; for it would be the hight of Folly and
Inconfideration, to defire ftill to flatter ourfelves,
and to remain quiet, in the expectation, that,
after the conclufion of the Peace, the Bufinefs,
at prefent turned out of its direction, fhould return entirely, into this country; for experience
fhews the contrary in a manner the moft convincing; and it is moft probable, that the fame
nations, who are actually in poffeffion of it, will
preferve, at that time, the greateft part of it.
Your alarmed Petitioners throw their eyes round

every where, to discover new fources, capable of
procuring them more fuccefs in future; they
even flatter themfelves, that they have found them
upon the new theatre of Commerce, which the
United States of America offer them; a Commerce, of which, in this moment, but in this moment only, they believe themfelves to be in a condition, to be able to affure to themfelves a good
fhare, and the great Importance of which, joined
to the fear of feeing escape from their hands
this only and laft Refource, has induced them to
take the refolution, to lay open refpectfully
their Obfervations, concerning this important object, to your High-Mightineffes, with the earneft
Prayer, that you would confider them with a ferious attention, and not interpret in ill part this
meafure of the Petitioners, efpecially as their future
wellbeing, perhaps even that of the whole Republick, depends on the decifion of this affair.

No man can call in queftion, that England has
derived her greateft forces from her Commerce
with America; thofe immenfe Treafures, which
that commerce has poured into the Coffers of the
State; the uncommon profperity of feveral of her
commercial Houfes, the extream Reputation of
her Manufactures, the Confumption of which, in
quantities beyond all bounds, contributes effica-
ciously to their Perfection, are convincing proofs
of it. However it may be, and notwithftanding
the fuppofition too lightly adopted, that we cannot
imitate the British Manufactures; the Manufac-
ture of painted Linnens of Rouen, thofe of wool
of Amiens, of Germany, of Overyffel, the Pins
of Zwoll, prove vifibly, that all things need not
be drawn from England; that, moreover, we are
as well in a condition, or fhall foon be, to equal
them in feveral refpects.

Per-

Permit us, high and mighty Lords, to the end
to avoid all further digreſſion, to requeſt in this
regard the attention of your high - Mightineſſes,
to the ſituation of Commerce in France at the
beginning of the war. Continual Loſſes had almoſt ruined it altogether like ours; ſeveral of her
Merchants failed of Capitals, and others wanted
courage to continue their Commerce; her Manufactures languiſhed; the People groaned; in one
word, every thing there marked out the hor-
rors of war. But, at preſent, her maritime Towns,
overpeopled, have occaſion to be enlarged; her
Manufactures having arrived at a degree of exportation unknown before, begin to perfect
themſelves more and more, in ſuch a degree, that
the melancholly Conſequences of the war are
ſcarcely felt in that Kingdom. But ſince it is in-
conteſtable, that this favourable alteration reſults
almoſt entirely from its Commerce with America, that even this has taken place in time of
war, which, moreover, is ever prejudicial, we
leave it to the enlightened Judgment of your High-
Mightineſſes, to decide, what it is that we may
expect from a Commerce of this nature, even at
preſent, but eſpecially in time of Peace. In the
mean time, we have had the happineſs to make a
tryal, of ſhort duration, it is true, but very
ſtrong in proportion to its continuance, in our
Colony of St. Euſtatia, of the importance of the
commerce, thò not direct, with North-America.
The Regiſters of the Weſt-India Company may
furniſh proofs of it very convincing to your High-
Mightineſſes; in fact, their Productions are infinitely ſuitable to our Market, whilſt, on our ſide,
we have to| ſend them ſeveral articles of Con-
venience and of Neceſſity from our own Coun-

D 4   try,

try, or from the neighbouring States of Germany.
Moreover, several of our languishing manufactures, scattered in the seven United Provinces,
may perhaps be restored to their former vigour, by means of Bounties, or the Diminution
of Imposts. The Importance of Manufactures for
a Country is sufficiently proved, by the considerable Gratifications promised and payed by British
Policy for their encouragement, and by the Advantages which that Kingdom has procured to
itself by this means, even beyond what had been
expected.

The Petitioners know perfectly well the obstacles, almost insurmountable, which always oppose themselves to the habitual use of new Manufactures, although certainly better in quality;
and they dare advance without hesitation, that several of our Manufactures are superiour to those
of the English : a moment more favourable can
never offer itself than the present, when by a Resolution of Congress the Importation of all the
effects of the Produce of Great Britain, and of
her Colonies, is forbidden ; which reduces the
Merchant and the Purchaser to the necessity of
recurring to other Merchandises, the use of which
will serve to dissipate the Prejudice conceived
against them. It is not only the Manufactures, high
and mighty Lords, which promise a permanent advantage to our Republick : the Navigation will derive also great advantages ; for it is very far from being
true (as several would maintain) that the Americans, being once in the tranquil possession of
their Independence, would themselves exercice
with vigour these two Branches, and that in the
sequel we shall be wholly frustrated of them.
Whoever has the least knowledge of the Country

try of America, and of its vaft Extent, knows
that the Number of Inhabitants is not there in
Proportion. That even the two Banks of the Mis-
fiffippi, the moft beautifull tract of this Country,
otherwife fo fertile, remain ftill uncultivated: and
as there are wanted fo many hands, it is not at
all probable to prefume, that they will or can
occupy themfelves to eftablish new Manufactures,
both becaufe of the new Charges; which are the-
reunto attached, and becaufe of the fhackles, which
they would put upon the Augmentation and Exportation of their Productions.

It is then for thefe fame reafons [the want
of Population) that they will fcarcely find the
hands neceffary to take advantage of the Fifheries, which are the Property of their Country;
which will certainly oblige them to abandon to
us the Navigation of Freight. There is not therefore any one of our Provinces, much lefs any one
of our Cities, which cannot enjoy the advantage
of this Commerce; No, High and mighty Lords,
the Petitioners are perfuaded that the utility and
the benefit of it, will fpread itfelf over all the
Provinces and Countries of the Generality.
Guelderland and Overysfel cannot too much ex-
tend their Manufactures of Wool, of Swanskin
and other things: even the Shoemakers of the
Mayoralty, and of Langftreet, will find a confiderable opening : almoft all the Manufactures of
Utrecht and of Leyden will flourish anew. Har-
lem will fee revive its Manufactures of Stuffs,
of Laces, of Ribbons, of Twift, at prefent in
the loweft ftate of decay. Delft will fee vaftly
augmented the fale of its Earthen ware, and
Gouda that of its Tabacco Pipes.

However great may be the advantages forefeen by the Petitioners, from a legal Commerce duely protected with America, their fear is not lefs, left we fhould fuffer to efcape the happy moment of affuring to them, and to all the Republick, thefe advantages. The prefent moment muft determine the whole. The English Nation is weary of the war, and as that People runs eafily into extreams, the Petitioners are afraid, with ftrong probable appearances, that a compleat acknowledgment of American Independance will foon take place; aboave all, if the English fee an opportunity of being able ftill to draw from America fome conditions favourable for them, or at leaft fomething to our difadvantage. Ah! what is it, which fhould inftigate the Americans, in making Peace, and renewing Friendship with Great Britain, to have any regard for the Interefts of our Republick? If England could only obtain for a Condition, that we fhould be obliged to pay Duties more burthenfome for our Veffels, this would be not only a continual and permanent Prejudice; but would be fufficient, to transmit to Pofterity a lamentable Proof of our exceffive Deference for unbridled Ennemies.

The Petitioners dare flatter themfelves, that a meafure fo frank of this Republick, may powerfully ferve for the Acceleration of a general Peace. A general ardour, to extinguish te flames of war, reigns in England; an upright and vigorous conduct, on the part of this Republick, will contribute to accelerate the accomplishment of the wishes for Peace.

We flatter ourfelves, High and Mighty Lords, that we have in this regard alledged fufficient reafons for an immediate decifion; and that we have fo vifibly proved the danger of Delay, that
we

we dare to hope from the paternal Equity of your
High-Mightineſſes, a reaſonable attention to the
reſpectfull Propoſition which we have made. It
proceeds from no other motive, than a ſincere
affection for the precious Intereſts of our dear
Country; ſince we conſider it as certain, that as
ſoon as the ſtep taken by us ſhall be known by
the Engliſh, and that they ſhall have the leaſt
hope of preventing us, they will not fail, as ſoon
as poſſible, to acknowledge American Independence.
Supported by all theſe reaſons, the Petitioners
addreſs themſelves to your Hihh-Mightinesſes,
humbly requeſting, that it may pleaſe your High-
Mightinesſes, after the occurrences and affairs above mentioned, to take, for the greateſt advantage of this Country, as ſoon as poſſible, ſuch Reſolution as your High-Mightineſſes ſhall judge
moſt convenient-

This doing &c.

PETITION

P E T I T I O N

to the Burgomasters and Regents of

A M S T E R D A M.

The Subscribers, all Merchants and Manufacturers of this City, with all due Respect, give to understand : That the Difference arisen
between the Kingdom of Great - Britain and the
United States of America, has not only given occasion for a long and violent war, but that the
arms of America have covered themselves with
a success so happy, that the Congress, assisted by
the Courts of France and Spain, have so well
established their Liberty and Independence, and
reduced Great Britain to extremities so critical,
that the House of Commons in England, notwithstanding all the oppositions of the British Ministry,
have lately formed the important Resolution, to
turn the King from an offensive war against America, with no other design than to accelerate, if
it is possible, a Reconciliation with America.

That to this happy Revolution in the dispo-
sitions of the English in favour of the Liberty and
Independence of America, according to all appearances, the Resolution taken by the Congress,
towards the end of the last year, to wit, to forbid in all America the Importation of British Manufactures and Productions, has greatly contributed : a Resolution, of which they perceive in England,

gland, too viſibly, the conſequences ruinous to
their Manufactures, Trades, Commerce, and Navigation, to be able to remain indifferent in this
regard. For all other commercial Nations, who
take to heart, ever ſo little, their own Proſperity, will apply themſelves ardently, to collect
from it all the fruit poſſible. To this effect, it
would be unpardonable for the Buſineſs and Commerce of this Republick in general, and for thoſe of
this City in particular, to ſuffer to eſcape this occaſion ſo favourable for the encouragement of
our Manufactures ſo declined, and languishing in
the interiour Cities, as well as that of the Commerce and Navigation in the maritime Cities; or
to ſuffer that other commercial Nations, even
with a total excluſion of the mercantile Intereſts
of this Republick, ſhould profit of it, and this
upon an occaſion, when, by reaſon of the war,
equally unjuſt and ruinous, in which the Kingdom
of Great · Britain has involved this Republick,
we cannot, and ought not to have the leaſt Regard or Condeſcenſion for that jealous State,
being able even to oblige this arrogant Neighbour,
in the juſt fear of the conſequences, which a more intimate Connection between this Republick
and North-America would undoubtedly have, to lay
down the ſooner her Arms, and reſtore Tranquility to all Europe.

That the Petitioners, notwithſtanding the Inclination they have for it, ought not nevertheleſs to explain themſelves farther upon this object, nor make a demonſtration in detail of the
important advantages, which this Republick may
procure itſelf by a Connection and a Relation more intimate with North · America; both becauſe
that no well-informed man can eaſily call the
thing

thing in queſtion, or contradict it; but alſo, becauſe the States of Friesland themſelves have very lately explained themſelves, in a manner ſo remarkable, in this reſpect; and which is ſtill more
remarkable, becauſe in very different Circumſtances, with a Foreſight, which Poſterity will cele-
brate by ſo much the more, as it is attacked in
our time by ill deſigning Citizens, the Lords your
Predeceſſors thought, four years ago, upon the
means of hindering this Republick from being excluded from the Buſineſs of the new World, and
from falling into the disagreable ſituation, in which
the Kingdom of Portugal is at preſent, conſidering
that, according to the Informations of your Petitioners, the Congreſs has excluded that Kingdom
from all Commerce and Buſineſs with North-
America, ſolely, becauſe it had perceived that it
ſuffered itſelf to be too ſtrongly directed by the
Influence of the British Court. This example makes us fear with reaſon, that if the Propoſitions
made, in the name of America, by Mr. Adams
to this Republick, ſhould remain, as they ſtil are,
without an anſwer, or that, if, contrary to all
expectation, they ſhould be rejected, in that Caſe the Republick ought not to expect a better
Treatment.

   That, for theſe reaſons and many others, the
Petitioners had flattered themſelves, that we
ſhould long ago have opened Negotiations, and
a cloſer Correſpondence, with the United States
of America. But this important work appeared
too meet with difficulties with ſome, as incom-
patible with the Acceſſion of this Republick to
the armed Neutrality, and in courſe, with the accepted Mediation; whilſt that others cannot be
Perſuaded to make this ſo neceſſary ſtep, in the
                                                  opi-

opinion, that we cannot draw any advantage, or
at least of much Importance, from a more strict
Connection with America: Reasons, according
to the Petitioners, the Frivolity of which is ap-
parent to every one, who is not filled with Prejudice, without having occasion to employ many
words to point it out. For, as to the first Point,
supposing for a moment, that it might be made a
question, whether the Republick, after her Accession to the armed Neutrality, before the war with
England could take a step of this nature, without
renouncing at the same time the Advantages of
the armed Neutrality, which it had embraced;
it is at least very certain, that every difficulty
concerning the Competency of the Republick to
take a similar step, vanishes and disappears of itself
at present, when it finds itself involved in a war
with Great-Britain, since from that moment she
could not only demand, the assistance and succour
of all the Confederates in the armed Neutrality,
but that thereby she finds herself authorized, for
her own defence, to employ all sorts of means,
violent and others, which she could not before
adopt nor put in use, while she was really in the
Position of a Neutral Power, which would profit of the advantages of the armed Neutrality.
This Reasoning then proves evidently, that in
the present situation of affairs, the Republick
might acknowledge the Independence of America, and notwithstanding this, claim of full right
the Assistance of her neutral Allies, at least, if we
would not maintain one of the two following ab-
surdities: that, notwithstaning the violent aggres-
sion of England in Resentment of our Accession
to the armed Neutrality, we dare not defend ourselves, untill our Confederates shall think proper
to

to come to our affiftance; or, otherwife, that
being attacked by the Englifh, it fhould be permitted us, conformably to the rights of the armed
Neutrality, to refift them in Arms, whether on
the Doggersbank or elfewhere, but not by con-
tracting Alliances, which certainly do no Injury
or harm to the Convention of the armed Neutrality, notwithftanding even the fmall hope we have of being fuccourred by the Allies of the armed
Confederation. The Argument of the Mediation
is ftill more contrary to common fenfe in this,
that it fuppofes, that the Republick, by accep-
ting the Mediation, has alfo renounced the Employment of all the means, by the way of Arms,
of Alliances, or otherwife, which it might judge
ufefull or neceffary to annoy her Ennemy: a fuppofition, which certainly is deftitute of all foundation, and which would reduce it fimply to a
real Sufpenfion of Hoftilities on the Part of the
Republick only; to which the Republick can never have confented, neither directly nor indi-
rectly.
Befides this laft Argument, the Petitioners ought
to obferve, in the firft place, that by means of a
good Harmony and Friendship with the United
States of America, there will fpring up, not only different Sources of Bufinefs for this Republick, founded folely on Commerce and Navigation, but in particular the Manufactures and Trade
will affume a new Activity in the interiour Cities;
for they may confume the amount of Millions
of our Manufactures in that new Country, of fo
vaft Extent: In the fecond Place, abftracted from
all Interefts of Commerce, the Friendship or the
Enmity of a Nation, which, after having made
Prifoners of two English Armies, has known how

to

to render herfelf refpectable and formidable, if it were only in relation to the weftern Poffeffions of
this State, is not and cannot be in any manner
indifferent for our Republick. In the laft place,
it is neceffary that the Petitioners remark farther in this refpect, that feveral Inhabitants of
this Republick, in the prefent fituation of affairs,
fuffer very confiderable Loffes and Damages, which
at leaft hereafter might be wholly prevented, or
in part, in cafe we fhould make with the United
States of America, with relation to Veffels and
Effects recaptured, a Convention fimilar to
that, which has been made with the Crown of France the laft year; for, venerable Regents, if a
Convention of this nature had been contracted,
in the beginning of this war, the Inhabitants of
the Republick would have already derived important advantages from it, confidering that feveral Ships and Cargoes, taken by the English
from the Inhabitants of this State, have fallen into the hands of the Americans; among others,
two Veffels from the Weft-Indies, richly loaded,
and making fail for the Ports of the Republick,
and both eftimated at more than a Million of Florins of Holland; which captured by the English
at the commencement of the year paft, were carried into North-America, where, after the Ca-
pitulation of General Cornwallis, they paffed from
the hands of the English into others.

That, although the Petitioners are fully convinced, that the Interefts of the Commerce of
this common Country, and of this City, have conftantly, but efpecially in thefe laft years, attracted,
and ftill attract every day, a great part of the Cares of the venerable Regency; neverthelefs, having

E

ving regard to the Importance of the affair, the
Petitioners have thought that they might, and that
they ought to take the Liberty, to address themselves with this Petition to you, venerable Regents, to inform you, according to truth, that the
moments are precious, that we cannot lose any
time, how little foever it may be, without running the greateſt risque of loſing all; ſince, by
heſitating longer, the Republick, according to all
appearances, would not derive any advantage, not
even more than it has derived from its acceſſion
to the armed Neutrality; becauſe that in the fear
of British menaces, we did not determine to ac-
ceed to it, untill the opportunity of improving
the advantage of it, was paſſed.

For theſe Cauſes, the Petitioners addreſs themſelves to you, venerable Regents, reſpectfully ſol-
liciting, that your efficacious Influence may con-
defcend, at the Aſſembly of their noble and grand
Mightineſſes the States of this Province, to direct
affairs in ſuch a manner, that upon this important object there may be taken as ſoon as poſſible, and, if poſſible, even during the continuance
of this Aſſembly, a final and deciſive Reſolution,
ſuch as you, venerable Regents and their noble
and grand Mightineſſes, according to their high
wisdom, ſhall judge the moſt convenient: and if,
contrary to all Expectation, this important operation ſhould meet with any obſtacle on the
part of one or more of the Confederates, that in
that caſe you, venerable Regents, in Concert
with the Province of Friesland, and thoſe of the
other Provinces, who make no difficulty to open
a Negotiation with America, will condeſcend to
confider of the means, which ſhall be found pro
per

per and convenient to effectuate, that the Commerce of this Province, as well as that of Friesland and the other Members adopting the same opinion, may not be prejudiced by any dilatory deliberations, nor too late resolved, for the Conclusion of a Measure as important as necessary.

So doing &c.

AMSTERDAM.

ADDRESS *of the Merchants', &c. to their Regency.*

NOBLE, GREAT, AND VENERABLE LORDS!

IT is for us a particular Satisfaction, to be able
to offer to your noble and great Lordships,
as Heads of the Regency of this City, this well
intentioned Address, that a multitude of our moſt
reſpectable fellow-Citizens have ſigned. It was already prepared and ſigned by many, when we learned,
as well by the publick Papers as otherwiſe, the
Propoſitions of a particular Peace, with an offer
of an immediate ſuſpenſion of Hoſtilities, on the
part of Great - Britain, made to this State by the
Mediation of the Ruſſian Ambaſſador. This is the
only reaſon, why no immediate mention was made
of it in the Addreſs itſelf. It is by no means the
idea, that theſe offers would have made any Im-
preſſion upon the Merchants; ſince we can, on
the contrary, in truth aſſure your noble and
great Lordships, that the unanimous ſentiment
nearly of the Exchange of Amſterdam, as much as
that is intereſted in it, is entirely conformable to
that, which the Merchants of Rotterdam have made known in ſo energic a manner: That conſequently we have the greateſt Averſion to like
offers, as artfull as dangerous, which being adopted, would very probably throw this Republick into other ſituations very embarraſſing, the immediate conſequences of which would be, to ruin it
total-

totally: whereas, on the other hand, thefe offers
fhew, that whe have only to deal with an Ennemy
exhaufted, whom we could force to a general and
durable Peace in the End, by following only the
example of France, Spain, and North-America,
and by ufing the means which are in our Hands.

It is improper for us, however, to enlarge further upon this Projeĉt, important as it may be,
being well affured, that your noble and great
Lordships fee thofe grievous Confequences more
clearly, than we can trace them.

The Merchants continue to recommend their
Commerce and Navigation to the conftant Care
and Proteĉtion of your noble and great Lordships,
and to infift only, that in cafe thefe offers of
the Court of England fhould be, at any time,
the Caufe, that the affair of the Admiffion
of Mr. Adams, in Quality of Minifter Plenipotentiary of the United States of America, fhould
meet with any difficulty or delay on the part of
the other Confederates, that your noble and great
Lordships, conformably to the fecond Article of
our Requifition, inferted in this Requeft, would
have the Goodnefs to think upon meafures, which
would fecure this Province from the ruinous Confequences of fuch a Proceeding.

*To the foregoing was joined the Addrefs prefented
to the Burgomafters and the Council, which is of the
following Tenor.*

NOBLE, GREAT, VENERABLE, AND NOBLE AND
VENERABLE LORDS!

The underfigned, Merchants, Citizens, and
Inhabitants of the City of Amfterdam, have
learned with an inexpreffible joy, the news of the

Res

Refolution taken the twenty-eighth of March laft
by their noble and grand Mightineffes, the Lords
the States of Holland and Weft-Friefland. Their
noble and grand Mightineffes have thereby, not
onle fatisfied the general wishes of the greateft
and beft part of the Inhabitants of this Province,
but they have laid the Foundations of ulteriour
Alliances and Correfpondencies of Friendship and
of good underftanding with the United States of
America, which promife new Life to the languishing ftate of our Commerce, Navigation and Manufactures. The Unanimity with which that Refolution was decided in the Affembly of Holland, gi-
ves us grounds to hope, that the States of the other
Provinces will not delay to take a fimilar Refolution; whilft the fame Unamity fills with the
moft lively Satisfaction the well intentioned Inhabitants of this City, and without doubt thofe of
the whole Country, in convincing them fully,
that the Union among the fage and venerable Fathers of the Country increafes more and more;
whilft that the Promptnefs and Activity, with
which it hath been concluded, make us hope,
with reafon, that we fhall reap, in time, from
a ftep fo important, and fo neceffary for this Republick, the defired Fruits. Who then can call
in queftion, or disavow, that the moment feems
to approach nearer and nearer, when this Republick fhall enter into new Relations with a People, which finds itfelf in Circumftances, which
differ but little from thofe in which our Ances-
tors found themfelves two Centuries ago; with a
People which conciliates more and more the general Affection and Efteem.

The Conformity of Religion and Government,
which is found between us and America, joined

to

to the indubitable Marks, that fhe hath already
long fince given of the Preference that fhe
feels for our Friendship, makes the underfigned
not only fuppofe, but infpire them with, a Confidence,
that our Conne&ions with her will be equally
folid, advantageous and falutary, to the Interefts of
the two Nations. The Wellbeing and Profperity,
which will very probably refult from them; the
Part which you, noble, great, venerable, and
noble and venerable Lords, have had in the Conclufion of a Refolution fo remarkable; the Con·
vi&ion that the venerable Council of this City
had of it, upon the Propofition of the noble,
great and venerable Lords almoft confented to, before the Requeft relative to this proje& prefented
not long fince to you, noble, great and venerable Lords, had come to the knowledge of the
Council; finally the Remembrance of that which
was done upon this matter in the year 1778, with
the beft Intentions and the moft laudable views,
finding itfelf at prefent crowned with an approbation as publick as it is general, indifpenfibly oblige the underfigned to approach you with this Addrefs; not only to congratulate you upon fo remarkable an Event, but to thank you at the fame
time, with as much zeal as folemnity, for all
thofe well intentioned Cares, and thofe well concerted Meafures, for that inflexible Attachment,
and that faithfull Adherence to the true Interefts of
the Country in general and of this City in particular,
which manifeft themfelves, in fo ftriking a manner,
in all the Proceedings and Refolutions of your
noble, great and venerable Lordships and of the
venerable Council of this City, and which certainly
will attra& the efteem and veneration of the lateft
Pofterity, when comparing the Annals and Events

E 4   of

of the prefent with thofe of former times, it fhall discover that Amfterdam might ftill boaft itfelf of poff:ffing Patriots , who dared facrifice generously all views of private Interefts , of Grandeur and Confideration, to the facred obligations that their Country requires of them.

We flatter ourf:lves, noble, great, venerable, noble and venerable Lords, that the prefent publick demonftration of our Esteem and Attachment, will be fo much the more agreable , as it is more rare in our Republick, and perhaps even it is without example, and as it is more proper to efface all the odious Impreffions that the Calumny and Malignity of the English Miniftry , not long ago fo fervilely adored by many , but whofe downfall is at prefent confummated , had endeavoured to fpread, particularly a little before and at the beginning of this war ; Infinuations, which have fince found Partifans in the United Provinces, among thofe who have not been ashamed to paint the Exchange of Amfterdam (that is to fay the moft refpectable and the moft ufefull part of the Citizens of this City, and at the fame time the principal fupport of the wellbeing of the United Provinces) as if it confifted in a gread part of a contemptible Herd of vile interefted fouls, having no other Object, than to give loofe to their avidity, and to their defire of amaffing Treafures, in defrauding the publick Revenues, and in transporting articles, againft the Faith of Treaties; Calumniators, who have had at the fame time, and have ftill, the audacity to affront the moft upright Regency of the moft confiderable City of the Republick, and to expofe it to publick Contempt, as if it participated by Connivance, and otherwife, in fo fhamefull a Commerce ; Infinuations

tions and Accufations, which have been fpread,
with as much falshood as wickednefs, and which
ought to excite fo much the more the Indigna-
tion of every fenfible Heart, when it is confidered,
that not only the Merchants of this City, but alfo
thofe of the whole Republick, have fo inviolably
refpeƈted the Faith of Treaties, that to the afto-
nishment of every impartial man, one cannot produce any Proofs, at leaft no fufficient Proofs, that
there hath ever been transported from this Country
Contrabande Merchandizes; whilft that the Con-
junƈture, in which Imputations of this kind have
been fpread, rendered the Proceeding ftill more
odious, feeing it has been done at an Epocha,
when the Commerce and Navigation of Amfterdam, and of the whole Republick, would have experienced the firft and almoft the only Attack of
an unjuft and perfidious Ally, for want of neces-
fary Proteƈtion, upon which you, noble, great,
venerable, and noble and venerable Lords, have
fo often and fo feriously infifted, even before the
commencement of the Troubles between Great-
Britain and the United States of America; at an
Epocha, when the Merchant, formed for enter-
prifes, was obliged to fee the fruit of his Labour,
and of his Cares, the recompence of his indefati-
gable, Induftry, and the Patrimony deftined to his
Pofterity, ravished from his hands by foreign
violence and an unbounded Rapacity; at an epocha finally, when the wife and prudent Politi-
cians, who had exhaufted themfelves and fpared
no pains for the publick Good, faw their patriotic
views diffipated, and their Projeƈts vanish.

Receive then, noble, great, venerable, and
noble and venerable Lords, this folemn Teftimony
of our lively Gratitude, as gracioufly, as it is

given

given sincerely on our part. Receive it as a Proof
of our Attachment to your Persons; an Attachment, which is not founded upon Fear, nor an
exteriour Representation of Authority, and Grandeur, but which is founded on more noble and
immoveable principles, those of esteem and Respect, arising from a sentiment of true Greatness
and of Generosity. Be assured, that when contemptible Discord, with its odious attendants
Artifice and Imposture, could effectuate nothing,
absolutely nothing, at the moment when the present war broke out, to prejudice in the least the
Fidelity of the Citizens of the Amstel, or to shake
them in the observance of their Duties, the In-
conveniences and the evils, that a war naturally
and necessarily draws after it, will not produce
the effect neither. Yes, we will submit more willingly to them, according as we shall perceive,
that the means, that God and Nature have put into
our Hands, are more and more employed to reduce and humble an haughty ennemy. Continue
then, noble, great, venerable, noble and venerable Lords, to proceed with safety in the Road
that you follow, the only one, which in our Opinion can, under the divine Benediction, tend to
save the Country from its present situation. Let
nothing divert or intimidate you from it. You have
already surmounted the greatest difficulties, and the
most poignant Cares. A more pleasing Perspective
already opens. Great Britain, not long since so
proud of her Forces, that she feared not to declare
war against an ancient and faithfull Ally, already
repents of that unjust and rash Proceeding; and,
succumbing under the weight of a war, which
becomes more and more burthensome, she sighs
after Peace, whilst that the Harmony among the
members

members of the fupream Government of this Country increafes with our Arms, according as your
political fyftem, whofe Neceffity and falutary Influence were heretofore lefs acknowledged, gains
every day more numerous Imitators. The Refolution lately taken by the States of Friesland,
and fo unanimously adopted by our Province, fur-
nishes, among many others, one inconteftible
Proof of it, whilft the naval Combat, fought the
laft year on Doggersbank, hath fhewn to aftonis-
hed Europe, that fo long a Peace, hath not made
the Republick forget the management of Arms,
but that on the contrary it nourishes in its Bofom
warriours, who tread in the footfteps of Tromps
and Ruiters, from whofe Prudence and Intrepidity,
after a Beginning fo glorious, we may promife ourfelves the moft heroic Actions; that their invin-
cible Courage, little affected with an evident fu-
periority, will procure one day to our Country an
honourable and permanent Peace, which, in
eternizing their military Glory, will caufe the wife
Policy of your noble, great, venerable, and noble
and venerable Lordships, to be bleffed by the lateft Pofterity.

UTRECHT

UTRECHT.

24. *April* 1782.

To their noble Mightinesses, the Lords
' the States of the Country of Utrecht.

THE underſigned Manufacturers, Merchants,
and other Traders of this City, give with
due reſpect to underſtand, that the Petitioners
placing their Confidence in the Intereſt ; that your
noble Mightineſſes have always appeared to ta‧
ke in the advancement of Manufactures and Com‧
merce, have not been at all ſcrupulous to recommend to the vigilant attention of your noble
Mightineſſes, the favourable occaſion that offers
itſelf in this moment, to revive the Manufactures,
Commerce and Trades fallen into decay in this
City and Province, in caſe that your noble Migh‧
tineſſes acknowledged, in the name of this City,
Mr. Adams as Miniſter Plenipotentiary of the United States of America, to the end that there might
be formed with them a Treaty of Commerce for
this Republick. As the Petitioners founded themſelves thus upon the intimate ſentiment of the
execution of that, which your noble Mightineſſes
judge proper to the advancement of the wellbeing of the Petitioners and of their Intereſts, the
Petitioners have further the ſatisfaction of ſeeing
the moſt agreable Proofs of it, when your noble
Mightineſſes, in your laſt Aſſembly, reſolved una-
nimouſly to conſent, not only to the admiſſion of
Mr.

Mr. Adams in quality of Minifter of the Congrefs,
of North-America, but to authorize the Lords the
Deputies of this Province at the Generality, to
conform themfelves in the name of this Province,
to the Refolutions of the Lords the States of
Holland and Weftfriesland and of Friesland, and
doing this, to confent to the acknowledgment and
admiffion of Mr. Adams, as Minifter of the United States of America. As that Refolution fur-
nifhes the Proofs the beft intentioned, the moft
patriotic, for the advancement of that which may
ferve to the wellbeing en to the encouragement of
Manufactures, of Commerce and of decayed Trades, as well in general, as of this City and Province in particular, and which had been fo ardently defired; the Petitioners thinck themfelves
indifpenfably obliged to teftify, in the moft refpectfull manner, their gratitude for it to your
noble Mightineffes. The Petitioners find themfelves abfolutely unable, to exprefs in words the general fatisfaction that this event hath caufed not
only to them, but alfo to the great and fmall of
this Province; joined to the confirmation of the
perfect Conviction in which they repofe themfelves
alfo, for the future, upon the paternal care of
your noble Mightineffes, that the Confummation
of the defired Treaty of Commerce with the Americans may be foon effected. The Petitioners at-
teft by the prefent, before your noble Mightinesfes, their folemn and well-meant Gratitude, which
they addrefs at the fame time to your noble
Mightinesfes, as the moft fincere mark of veneration and refpect for the Perfons, and the direction
of publick affairs, of your noble Mightineffes ;
praying that Almighty God may deign to blefs the
Efforts, and the Councils of your noble Mightineffes,

neffes, as well as thofe of the Confederates; that
moreover this Province, and our dear Country,
by the Propofitions of an Armiftice and that which
depends thereon, fhould not be involved in any
Negotiations for a particular Peace with our
perfidious Ennemy, but that we obtain no other
Peace than a general Peace, which (as your noble Mightineffes exprefs yourfelves in your Refolution) may be compatible with their Honour
and Dignity; and ferve not only for this Gene-
ration, but alfo for the lateft Pofterity, as a Monument of Glory, of eternal Gratitude, to and
efteem for the Perfons and public Adminiftration
of the prefent time.

FRIESLAND.

F R I E S L A N D.

E X T R A C T *from the Regifter - Book of the Lords the States of Friesland.*

THE Requifition of Mr. Adams, for prefen-
ting his Letters of Credence from the United States of America to their High-Mightinesfes, having been brought into the Affembly, and
put into deliberation, as alfo the ulteriour Addrefs
to the fame Purpofe, with a demand of a categorical anfwer, made by him, as is more amply mentioned in the minutes of their High-Mightineffes
of the 4th. of May 1781 , and the 9th. of January
1782; whereupon it having been taken into Confideration, that the faid Mr. Adams would probably have fome Propofitions to make to their
High-Mightineffes , and to prefent to them the
principal Articles and Foundations upon which the
Congrefs, on their part, would enter into a Treaty of Commerce and Friendfhip, or other affairs
to propofe, in regard to which difpatch would be
requifite.

It has been thought fit and refolved, to authorize the Lords the Deputies of this Province at
the Generality, and to inftruct them, to direct
things, at the Table of their High - Mightinesfes, in fuch a manner, that the faid Mr. Adams
be admitted forthwith as Minifter of the Congrefs of North-America; with further order to the
faid Deputies, that if there fhould be made moreover any fimilar Propofitions by the fame, to
in-

inform immediately their noble Mightineffes of them. And an Extract of the prefent Refolution fhall be fent them for their Information, that they may conduct themfelves conformably.

Thus refolved at the Province-Houfe the 26 February 1782.

Compared with the aforefaid Book to my knowledge.

Signed

A. J. V. SMYNIA.

HOLLAND

H O L L A N D

A N D

WESTFRIESLAND.

EXTRACT *of the Refolutions of the Lords the States of Holland and Weftfriesland, taken in the Affembly of their Noble and Grand-Mightineffes, Thursday* 28 *March* 1782.]

DELIBERATED by Refumption upon the Addrefs and the ulteriour Addrefs of Mr. Adams, made the 4th. of May 1781, and the 9th of January 1782, to the Prefidẹnt of the States General, communicated to the Affembly the 9 May 1781, and the 22d. of laft Month, to prefent his Letters of Credence, in the name of the United States of America, to their High-Mightineffes; by which ulteriour Addrefs, the faid Mr. Adams hath demanded a categorical anfwer, that he may acquaint his Conftituents thereof: deliberated alfo upon the Peti:ions of a great number of Merchants, Manufacturers and other Inhabitants of this Province, interefted in Commerce to fupport their Requeft prefented to the States General, the twentyeth current, to the end, that efficacious Meafures might be taken to eftablish a Commerce between this Country and North-America, Copy of which Petitions have been given to the Members the twenty firft; it hath been thought fit

F   and

and refolved, that the affair fhall be directed on the part of their noble and grand Mightineffes, at the Affembly of the States General, and that fhall be there made the ftrongeft Inftances, that Mr. Adams be admitted and acknowledged, as foon as poffible, by their High-Mightineffes, in quality of Ambaffador of the United States of America. And the Councellor Penfionary hath been charged to inform under hand the faid Mr. Adams of this Refolution of their noble and grand Mighti‐ neffes.

ZEALAND.

ZEALAND.

EXTRACT *of the Resolutions of their High-
Mightinesses the States General of the United
Provinces. Monday 8 April 1782.*

THE Deputies of the Province of Zealand
have brought to the Assembly, and have cau-
sed to be read there, the Resolution of the States
of the said Province, their Principals, to cause to
be admitted, as soon as possible, Mr. Adams in
quality of Ambassador of the Congress of North-
America, according to the following Resolution.

EXTRACT *from the Register of the Resolutions
of the Lords the States of Zealand, 4th. of
April 1782.*

It hath been thought fit and ordered, that the
Lords, the ordinary Deputies of this Province at
the Generality, shall be authorised, as it is done
by the present, to assist, in the direction of affairs
at the Assembly of their High-Mightinesses, in such
a manner, that Mr. Adams may be acknowledged,
as soon as possible, as Ambassador of the Congress
of North-America; that his Letters of Credence
be accepted; and that he be admitted in that quality, according to the ordinary form; enjoining
further upon the said Lords the ordinary Deputies, to take such Propositions, as should be made to this Republick by the said Mr. Adams, for

F 2   the

the Information and Deliberation of their High-
Mightinesses, to the end to transmit them here
as foon as possible. And an Extract of this Refolution of their noble Mightinesses shall be sent to
the Lords their ordinary Deputies, to serve them
as an Instruction.

Signed

J. M. CHALMERS.

Upon which having deliberated, it hath been
thought fit and resolved, to pray by the present
the Lords the Deputies of the Province of Guelderland, Utrecht, and Groningen and Ommelanden, who have not yet explained themselves upon
this subject, to be pleased to do it as foon as
possible.

OVERYSSELL.

OVERYSSEL.

EXTRACT *from the Register of the Resolutions of the Equestrian Order, and of the Cities compofing the States of Overyffel. Zwoll 5 April 1782.*

MR. the grand Bailiff of Saalland, and the other Commiffioners of their noble Mightineffes for the Affairs of Finance, having examined, conformably to their Commifforial Refolution of the third of this month, the Addreffes of Mr. Adams, communicated to the Affembly the 4th. of May 1781, and the 22 of February 1782, to prefent his Letters of Credence to their High Mightineffes, in the name of the United States of America; as well as the Refolution of the Lords the States of Holland and Weftfriesland dated the 28th. of March 1782, carried the 29th. of the fame Month to the Affembly of their High-Mightineffes, for the admiffion and acknowledgment of Mr. Adams, have reported to the Affembly, that they fhould be of opinion, that the Lords the Deputies of this Province in the States General ought to be authorifed and charged, to declare in the Affembly of their High-Mightineffes, that the Equeftrian order and the Cities judge, that it is proper to acknowledge, as foon as poffible, Mr. Adams in quality of Minifter of the United States of North-America to their High-Mightineffes. Upon which having deliberated, the Equeftrian Order and the Cities have conformed themfelves to the faid Report.

Compared with the aforefaid Regifter.

Signed   DERK DUNBAR

GRONINGEN.

*E*XTRACT *from the Regiſter of the Reſolutions of their noble Mightineſſes, the States of Groningen and Ommelanden. Tuesday* 9 *April* 1782.

THE Lords the States of Groningen and Om-melanden, having heard the Report of the Lords the Commiſſioners for the Petitions of the Council of State and the Finances of·the Provin-ce, and having carefully examined the demand of Mr. Adams, to preſent his Letters of Credence from the United States of America to their High-Mightineſſes, have, after deliberation upon the ſubject, declared themſelves of opinion, that in the critical circumſtances in which the Republick finds itſelf at preſent, it is proper to take, with-out loſs of Time, ſuch efficacious meaſures, as may not only repair the Loſſes and Damages, that the Kingdom of Great-Britain hath cauſed in a manner ſo injuſt, and againſt every ſhadow of Right, to the Commerce of the Republick, as well before as after the war, but particularly ſuch as may eſtablish the free Navigation and the Commerce of the Republick, for the future, upon the moſt ſolid Foundations, as may confirm and reaſſure it, by the ſtrongeſt Bonds of reciprocal Intereſt ; and that, in conſequence, the Lords the Deputies at the Aſſembly of their High-Migh-tineſſes ought to be authoriſed, on the part of the Province, as they are by the preſent, to ad-mit Mr. Adams to preſent his Letters of Credence,

ce from the United States of America, and to receive the Propofitions which he fhall make, to make Report of them to the Lords te States of this Province.

Signed

E. LEWE, *Secretary.*

The States General, having deliberated the fame day upon the Refolution, have refolved, that the Deputies of this Province of Guelderland, which has not yet declared itfelf upon the fame fubject, fhould be requefted, to be pleafed to do it as foon as poffible.

UTRECHT.

EXTRACT *of the Refolutions of their noble Migh-tineſſes, the States of the Province of Utrecht.* 10 *April* 1782.

HEARD the Report of Mr. DeWeſterveld and other Deputies of their noble Mightineſſes for the department of war, who, in virtue of the commiſſorial Reſolutions of the 9 May 1781, 16 January and 20 March of the preſent year 1782, have examinated the Reſolutions of their High-Mightineſſes of the 4 May 1781, containing an overture, that Mr. the Preſident of the Aſſembly of their High-Mightineſſes had made ,, that a Perſon ſtyling himſelf J. Adams had been with him, and had given him to underſtand, that he had recei-ved Letters of Credence for their High-Mightineſſes from the United States of America, with a requeſt, that he would be pleaſed to communi-cate them to their High-Mightineſſes; as well as the Reſolution of their High Mightineſſes of the 9 January, containing an ulteriour overture of Mr. the Preſident ,, that the ſaid Mr. Adams had been with him, and had inſiſted upon a categorical anſwer, whether his ſaid Letters of Credence would be accepted or not; finally the Reſolution of their High-Mightineſſes of the 5 of March laſt, with the Inſertion of the Reſolution of Friesland, containing a propoſition to admit Mr. Adams in quality of Miniſter of the Congreſs of North-America ".

Upon

Upon which having deliberated, and remarked,
that the Lords the States of Holland and Westfriesland, by their Resolution carried the 29 of
March to te States General, have also consented
to the admission of the said Mr. Adams in quality, of Minister of the Congress of North-America, it hath been thought fit and resolved, that the
Lords the Deputies of this Province in the States
General should be authorised, as their noble
Mightinesses authorise them by the present, to conform themselves, in the name of this Province,
to the Resolution of the Lords the States of Holland
and Westfriesland, and of Friesland, and to con-
sent by consequence, that Mr. Adams be acknowledged and admitted as Minister of the United States of America; their noble Mightinesses being at
the mean time of opinion, that it would be necessary
to acquaint her Majesty the Empress of Russia,
and the other Neutral Powers, with the Resolution
to be taken by their High-Mightinesses upon this
subject, in communicating to them, as much as
shall be necessary; the Reasons, which have induced their High-Mightinesses to it, and giving them
the strongest assurances, that the Intention of their
High-Mightinesses is by no means to prolong thereby the war, which they would have willingly prevented and terminated long since; but on the contrary, that their High-Mightinesses wish nothing
with more ardor, than a prompt Reestablishment
of Peace; and that they shall be always ready on
their part, to co-operate in it in all possible ways,
and with a suitable Readiness, so far as that shall
be any way compatible with their Honour and their
Dignity, and for this end an Extract of this shall
be carried by Missive to the Lords the Deputies
at the Generality.

F 5   GUEL.

GUELDERLAND.

EXTRACT *from the Recès of the ordinary Diet, held in the City of Nimeguen, in the Month of April* 1782. *Wednesday,* 17 *April* 1782.

THE Requifition of Mr. Adams, to prefent his Letters of Credence to their High - Mightinesfes in the name of the United States of America, having been brought to the Affembly and read, as well as an ulteriour Addrefs made upon this fubject, with a demand of a categorical anfwer by the faid Mr. Adams, more amply mentioned in the Regifters of their High-Mightineffes of the date of the 4th. of May 1781, and of the 9 January 1782; moreover the Refolutions of the Lords the States of the five other Provinces, carried fucceffively to the Affembly of their High-Mightineffes, and all tending to admit Mr. Adams in quality of Ambaffador of the United States of America to this Republick; upon which their noble Mightineffes, after Deliberation, halve refolved to authorize the Deputies of this Province at the States General, as they authorize them by the prefent, to conform themfelves in the name of this Province to the Refolution of the Lords the States of Holland and Weftfriesland, and to confent by confequence, that Mr. Adams may be acknowledged and admitted in quality of Ambaffador of the United States of America to this Republick. In confequence, an Extract of the
pre-

prefent fhall be fent to the faid Deputies, to make as foon as poffible the requifite overture of it to the Affembly of their High-Mightineffes.

In fidem Extracti.

Signed

J. In de Betouw.

THE

THE
STATES GENERAL.

EXTRACT *from the Regifter of the Refolutions of their High - Mightineffes the States General of the United Provinces. Fryday 19 April 1782.*

DELIBERATED by Refumption, upon the Addrefs and the ulteriour Addrefs, made by Mr. Adams the 4 May 1781, and the 9 January of the currant year to Mr. the Prefident of the Affembly of their High-Mightineffes, to prefent to their High - Mightineffes his Letters of Credence in the name of the United States of North-America; and by which ulteriour Addrefs the faid Mr. Adams hath demanded a categorical anfwer, to the end to be able to acquaint his Conftituents thereof; it hath been thought fit and refolved, that Mr. Adams fhall be admitted and acknowledged in quality of Ambaffador of the United States of North-America to their High-Mightineffes, as he is admitted and acknowledged by the prefent.
  Signed
   W. BOREEL, *Prefidt.*
 Lower down
  Compared with the aforefaid Regifter.
   Signed
    H. FAGEL.

EXTRACT

EXTRACT *from the Register of the Resolutions*
of their High-Mightinesses the States General
of the United Provinces, Monday 22 *April* 1782.

MR. BOREEL, who presided in the Assembly the last weak, hath reported to their
High-Mightinesses, and notified them, that Mr
John Adams, Ambasfador of the United States of
America, had been with him last Saturday, and
presented to him a Letter from the Affembly of
Congress, written at Philadelphia the first of January 1781, containing a Credence: for the said
Mr. Adams, to the end to reside in quality of
its Minister Plenipotentiary near their High-Mightinesses: Upon which having deliberated, it hath
been thought fit and resolved, to declare by the
present: ,, That the said Mr. Adams is agreable
,, to their High-Mightinesses; that he shall be
,, acknowledged in quality of Minister Plenipo-
,, tentiary; and that there shall be granted to him
,, an Audience, or affigned Commissioners, when
,, he shall demand it ". Information of the
above shall be given to the said Mr. Adams,
by the Agent van der Burch de Spieringshoek.

    Signed
        W. VAN CITTERS;, *Presidt.*
  Lower down
        Compared with the aforesaid Register.
              Signed
                H. FAGEL.

MEDAL.

M E D A L.

THE Society of Citizens, eſtabliſhed at Leeuwarden, under the Motto: „By Liberty and
„ Zeal", moſt humbly repreſents, that it deſires
to have an opportunity of teſtifying publickly,
by Facts, to your noble Mightineſſes the moſt lively, but, at the ſametime, the moſt reſpectfull
ſentiments of gratitude, which not only animate
them, but alſo, as they aſſure themſelves, all the
well intentioned Citizens, eſpecially, with relation to the Reſolutions equally important , and
full of wisdom, which your noble Mightineſſes
have taken upon all the Points, in regard to which
the critical Circumſtances, in which the dear Country finds itſelf plunged, have furniſhed to your noble Mightineſſes objects equally numerous and disagreable, particularly, at the ordinary Diet of the
year 1782, and at the extraordinary Diet held in
the Month of April laſt: Reſolutions which bear
not only the characters of wiſdom, but alſo thoſe
of the beſt intentioned ſollicitude, and the pureſt
Love of our Country; and which prove in the
moſt convincing manner, that your noble Mightineſſes have no greater ambition, than its univer-
ſal Proſperity; aſſiduouſly propoſing to yourſel-
ves, as the moſt important object of your attention, of your entrepriſes, and of your attachment,
the Rule: *Salus Populi ſuprema lex eſto*: Reſolutions, in fine, which ought perfectly to re-aſſure

the

the good Citizens of this Province, and encourage
them to perfevere in that full and tranquil Confidence, which has hindered them from reprefen-
ting to your noble Mightinesfes the true Interefts
of the Country, and to exhort them, at the fame time, by their fupplications, to act with courage, and to fullfill their Duties, confidering that
the faid Refolutions have fully affured them, that
their Poffeffions, with that which is above all
things dear to them, their Liberty (that Right
which is more precious to them than their Lives;
to which the fmalleft Injury cannot be done, without doing wrong and dishonour to Humanity; a
Right, neverthelefs, which, if we confider the
world in general, has been, alafs, almoft every
where equally violated) are depofited in fafety,
under the vigilant eye of your noble Mightineffes.
The Society has thought, that it might accom-
plish its wishes, in the moft convenient and de-
cent manner, in caufing to be ftruck, at its expence, a Medal of Silver, which may remain to
Pofterity a durable Monument of the perfect Harmony which at the prefent dangerous epocha has
reigned between the Government and the People.
It has conceived, for this purpofe, a Sketch or
Project, as yet incompleat, according to which
one of the fides of the Medal fhould bear the
Arms of Friesland, held by an hand, which de-
fcends from the Clouds, with an Infcription in
the following Terms: *To the States of Friesland, in
gratefull Memory of the Diets of February and of April
1782, dedicated by the Society* LIBERTY AND ZEAL.
An Infcription, which would thus contain a general applaufe of all the Refolutions taken in thefe
two Diets; whilft upon the Reverfe, one fhould
diftinguish, more particularly, the two Events,
which

which intereſt the moſt our common Country, in regard of which your noble Mightineſſes have given the Exemple to the States of the other Provinces, and which merit for this reaſon, as placed in the foremoſt ſituation, to ſhew itſelf the moſt clearly to the ſight : to wit „ The Admiſſion of Mr. Adams in quality of Miniſter of the United States of America to this Republick; and the Refuſal of a ſeparate Peace with Great-Britain". Events which ſhould be repreſented ſymbolically by a Friſian, dreſſed according to the ancient charaſteriſtick Cuſtom of the Friſians, holding out his right hand to an Inhabitant of North-America, in token of Friendſhip and Brotherly Love; whilſt with the left hand he rejeſts the Peace, which England offers him. The whole with ſuch convenient additions, and ſymbolical ornaments, which the Society, perhaps, would do well to leave to the Invention of the Medalliſt, &c.

[*The remainder of this Requeſt relates to other ſubjeſts.*]

Done at Leeuwarden the 8 May 1782.

The Society „ BY LIBERTY AND ZEAL".

Signed at its Requeſt

W. WOPKENS,

in the abſence of the Secretary.

✻ ✻ ✻

✻ ✻

✻